Now That I'm a Man

It takes a lot to be a man

Darryll D. Harmon

Cover Photo Credit:
Harry Glenn Sr.

Ronald Alexander

Stacey Brooks

Left to Right Top Row:
Dewitt R. Harmon Sr., Novak Mitchell, Morris Money, William "Bill" Thurman, Harry Glenn Sr., Howard Jackson, Clifton Powell

Left to Right Kneeling:
Al Easley, Mike C. Henry, James Jordan

DEDICATION

For years, I have longed to have this conversation with my son. This book is my way of beginning it. Nothing in this world means more to me than your peace of mind, your strength in body, and your light in spirit. Within these pages are lessons and experiences—some hard, some humbling—that I pray will guide you, shape you, and help you stand firm as you grow, be, and become the man you were meant to be.

CONTENTS

FOREWORD

The title of this book is ***Now That I'm a Man,*** with the subtitle ***It Takes a Lot to Be a Man.*** This work explores the many layers of manhood as I have experienced and observed it—not as a separation from the narrative of manhood, whether one views that narrative as good or bad, but as an honest contribution to the conversation. I am not writing from the outside looking in; I am in this story with you. My goal is not to assign blame but to expand the range of solutions available to us. The path to manhood is not one-size-fits-all, and what works for one man may not work for another—especially at different times in life.

Throughout these pages, I touch on many aspects of being a man. I examine the experiences of men from different ethnic backgrounds, ages, and stages of life—and the consistent themes that bind us all. I reflect on the complicated relationship between men and their families, their communities, and society at large.

I delve into the intersections of manhood and politics, highlighting how societal pressures, public policy, and political narratives shape our identities and choices. I also address manhood in the context of religion and spirituality—not promoting any one belief but encouraging reflection on how faith or personal values can influence one's growth and responsibilities.

Financial literacy and generational wealth are also at the heart of this discussion. It is not enough to succeed for ourselves; we must also consider what we leave behind for those who come after us. Manhood, in many ways, is about stewardship—of our resources, our relationships, and our reputations.

This book is a conversation. It's an invitation to think, to question, and most importantly, to evolve. You will find stories, reflections, and real-life situations that ask you not only to consider your role as a man but also to ask yourself what kind of man you want to be.

ACKNOWLEDGMENTS

1ST BALLOT HALL OF FAMER

(not in any order)

Dewitt Roland Harmon Sr.

Daniel Henry Sr.

Eddie Russell

Larry Soares Sr.

James Brown

Dewitt Roland Harmon Jr.

Derrick Roland Harmon

Eric Johnson Sr.

Eliot Walker Sr.

Ernie Garvins

James Jordan

Thomas Miles

Richard Wargo

Rev. Ellis B. Louden

Joseph Wright

David Daniels

Raymond Leary

Harry Glen Sr.

Daniel C. Henry Jr.

Daniel C. Henry Sr.

Carl Henry Sr.

Scott Bailey

Pastor Tyrone P. Jones

Johnny Johnson

William Thurman

John Henry Sr.

Alex Emond

Mr. Napoli

Bruce Posey

Charlie Tisdale

Rev. Johnny Gamble

William Smith Sr.

Pharaoh Paige

Guy Murray

John Mosley

Ricky Lyles

James Parker

Roosevelt Bradshaw Sr.

Coach Frank Brown

Brandon Dillahunt

Brian Cauthen

Ernest Nathan

Pablo Velez

Albert Emond

Joseph Henry

Jaime Ayinde

Rodney Blockum

Raymond Leary

Barry Banks

I'M 18, I'M AN ADULT

It must have been 1991 or 1992. I can't recall the exact scenario, but I'll never forget the moment my cousin Larry, in a burst of frustration, balled his fists, threw them down to his sides, and shouted with absolute conviction, "I'm 18, and I'm an adult!" Little did he know what lay ahead.

Like most teenagers, we were eager to get to the so-called finish line of adolescence and cross into the field of adulthood. In the United States, turning 18 legally marks that transition. But let me tell you something—you newly liberated 18-year-old: at some point, you'll probably wish you were a kid again. Don't be so quick to beat your chest about being grown.

I got it. By now, you may already have your driver's license, maybe even a job with your own money. You've been coming home late the weekends, no longer getting yelled at. You decide whether you're going to church and family event, not because your parents make you, but because it's your call. Many of the restrictions you've lived under are starting to fade.

For some young men, reaching 18 means stepping into roles their absent fathers never filled. Some have already had run-ins with the law. Others may be preparing to join the military. For some, 18 brings freedom; for others, it brings weight.

Whatever your situation, take a deep breath and trust the process of doing things the right way. When I say "right," I don't mean there's a perfect playbook—but there are principles. Stay within the limits of the law. Don't be so eager to prove your independence that you end up sabotaging your future. You may feel emboldened at home, ready to push back against rules. But if you still live under your parents' roof, understand—you're still subject to house rules. That doesn't make you less grown, it makes you respectful.

If you're looking to escape what you see as restrictions, going away to college might seem like the answer. Just make sure you're going for the right reasons. There's a cost to college—financial and emotional. While student loans may seem distant now, they will come due. That's why you should explore grants and scholarships to lighten the load.

Even though you're legally an adult, you don't have it all figured out—and that's okay. Be open to corrections. Try new things. Learn as much as you can. Don't measure your progress by what your friends have accomplished. Everyone's road is different.

I remember when I first moved to Charlotte. I used GPS to get around, choosing local streets so I could familiarize myself with the area. Later, I began taking the highways. What surprised me was that the travel time wasn't much different. The same is true for life. Your route to success might take longer, but the journey still counts.

Not everyone is built for college—and that's okay, too. Graduation from high school is a big deal. Whether you take a gap year or go straight into the workforce, stay productive. I went to trade school and studied carpentry, eventually joining the carpenters union. Trades like electrical, plumbing, culinary, and auto mechanics are valuable, sustainable careers. Give your best to whatever you choose.

You may try something and realize it's not for you. That's okay. Keep an open mind and do your research. Talk to professionals in different fields. With the rise of automation and artificial intelligence, be strategic about career paths.

While navigating 18 and beyond, get into the habit of saving—especially if you're still allowed to live at home. And yes, I say "allowed" because if you refuse to follow your parents' rules, you may be asked to leave. If you can, stay home as long as possible. It will help you build a financial cushion. And if you go away to college, don't burn bridges—you might need to come back.

Don't rush to adulthood. Don't jump into moving in with a girlfriend or having children just because you think it makes you grown. Children are a blessing, but they'll require you to grow up fast. If you're already in that situation, embrace it. Take care of your responsibilities and lean on family and friends who are willing to help. Raising a child still takes a village. Most of that concept is lost these days, but the theory and results have not changed.

Avoid debt as much as you can. There's a difference between good debt and bad debt. If you haven't read my first book, I encourage you to do so—I talk in depth about credit and cash flow. Over the next five to seven years, focus on creating cash flow. That's what sets you free.

Don't fall into the trap of car payments and high credit card bills. Think about it, most 18-year-olds don't even have high-paying jobs yet. Be mindful of your wants versus your needs. Learn to save. Make small, smart investments when opportunities arise.

Whatever you choose to do now that you're 18, do it with a healthy balance of work and fun. This is your time to establish what your version of work-life balance looks like. There may never be another time in your life when you have this much flexibility.

And if you feel stuck or don't know where to begin, visit a career center. Talk to family. Go back to your high school and schedule time with a guidance counselor. Not everyone will have access to the same resources—so be creative. Keep an open mind.

Don't be afraid to take entry-level jobs just to get your foot in the door. Many successful people started from the bottom.

You're 18 now—yes, you're an adult. But adulthood isn't about a number. It's about responsibility, maturity, and growth. Take your time, walk in wisdom, and build a future you'll be proud of.

A Hard Head Makes a Soft Ass

As the old saying goes, "A hard head makes a soft ass." This isn't just a warning—it's a life lesson. It means that when someone refuses to listen to wisdom or guidance, consequences will do the teaching instead. Many young men, driven by pride or surrounded by poor influences, reject mentorship and discipline. They believe they have to figure it all out on their own, that pain is the only path to growth. But pain is a harsh teacher. As my grandfather use to tell me don't learn the hard way, just listen to what people tell you.

Do not rely on only one way to view things; be open to other perspectives, other ways of handling changes and issues.

Now we know that in some cases, no male role model, mentor, or coach was available. Maybe your life situation didn't include structure or someone to teach you morals and values directly. Not everyone comes up in the same conditions, and that matters. But regardless of your starting point, life will still expect you to do some simple things—like take responsibility for your actions. That expectation doesn't change just because your circumstances were harder. The world still demands accountability. There are things in place for those who want to get away with taking responsibility for their actions.

Responsibility is not something that magically appears with age; it's a decision. When a man begins to take ownership of his actions—good or bad—he starts stepping into manhood. Being responsible doesn't mean you never make mistakes. It means you own them when you do. That awareness leads to accountability. And accountability leads to change.

When you are aware of how your actions impact your family, your community, and your future, you start to make different choices. You begin to recognize the patterns that lead to harm and understand that real power lies in restraint, in walking away, in saying no. That's when the shift begins—from a life of reacting to a life of responding.

Part of that shift is learning to admit when you're wrong, or when you simply don't know. There is strength in humility. Too many people fake knowledge or double down on poor decisions because they're afraid of looking weak. But the real weakness is pretending. Owning your mistakes or confessing that you don't have all the answers opens the door to learning, growth, and respect from those around you.

Growth starts with honesty—honesty with yourself. You don't need to be perfect to be respected. What people respond to is transparency and the willingness to grow. Saying "I messed up" or "I don't know, but I'm willing to learn" builds trust and character in ways that acting like you've got it all together never can.

Awareness sharpens your vision. Suddenly, you can see the long game, not just the moment you're in. You begin to weigh the cost of your actions before you commit to them. That moment of pause—of clarity—is where growth takes root. That's when you realize that every choice is a seed, and what you plant today will be the fruit you harvest tomorrow.

You also begin to realize that the ego is loud, but wisdom is quiet. The world may cheer for the fighter, but it remembers the man who brought peace. That might mean removing yourself from toxic environments, setting boundaries with people you once followed, or choosing not to escalate a situation when pride says otherwise.

This doesn't mean you're perfect. It means you're progressing. And progress, no matter how slow, is still movement in the right direction.

You have to be comfortable taking advice—even if you don't always use it. Advice is like a tool in your toolbox. You might not need it today, but it might save you tomorrow. Get addicted to hearing wisdom from others. Talk to older men, mentors, even peers who have been through some things. Listen more than you speak. You don't have to apply every piece of advice, but you should always be collecting it.

And while you're taking in what others say, make sure you're also taking into account your own self. Look at home—how you're living, how you're thinking, how you're treating the people closest to you. If the people in your home can't trust you, then the world doesn't owe you that either. Change starts closest to you and moves outward. If you want peace out there, you've got to bring order in here—right in your own house, your own habits, your own heart.

The goal is not to avoid all pain but to avoid unnecessary pain. Listen to the people trying to help you. Learn from the warnings. Don't let stubbornness be your downfall. You can be hard-headed and still be wise. You can be strong and still take advice. Because in the end, the softest blow is the one you dodge with wisdom, not endure with pride.

Bronny Is Ready, and So Are You

Bronny James. I'm sure you've heard the name—well, let me help you out. Bronny James is the oldest son of LeBron James, the all-time leading scorer in the NBA. LeBron has broken a multitude of records—first the youngest to accomplish so many things, and now, the oldest to maintain such dominance. LeBron came straight out of high school into the NBA and was often referred to as a "man-child" for his physical stature. He married his high school sweetheart, who continues to support him and their family in all that he does.

And now, we watch as Bronny charts his own course. While his journey will naturally draw comparisons to his father's, it is uniquely his own. Bronny may not have entered the league with the same fanfare, but that doesn't negate his readiness or potential. The foundation laid by LeBron—through work ethic, discipline, and example—has given Bronny tools that can't be measured solely by stats or draft pick numbers. In the workplace or in life, readiness isn't about perfection; it's about preparation, and Bronny has been preparing his whole life.

LeBron is, in my opinion, one of the most debated athletes of all time. Yet, ironically, he rarely gives anyone anything negative to talk about. Unlike many other athletes or public figures, including those who have held the highest offices in the land, LeBron has never been involved in a scandal that stained his legacy. Some would argue that those who critique LeBron are simply haters. I've lived long enough to witness countless public figures—actors, athletes, politicians—fall from grace due to proven misdeeds. But this chapter isn't about them.

The current debate centers around Bronny James, the eldest of LeBron's three children, and whether or not he's NBA ready. Let's break it down: Bronny averaged just 5 points in college and wasn't the best on his team although he did have a serious heart condition that prevented him from playing and working out.

The NBA is a job. Players are paid to take care of their bodies, to show up on time, to be team players, to study film and plays, and to represent the organization at all times. They are not paid to show up intoxicated or bring chaos into the workplace. They're paid to perform and uphold a standard. Think about it—certain professions that come with higher expectations. We wouldn't expect the president of a company to be embroiled in a scandal involving sexual misconduct. Nor would we want an elected official stealing from the very town they swore to serve.

Did LeBron influence his current team, the Los Angeles Lakers, to draft his son? No one really knows—and if he did, so what? Since when did we stop wanting the very best for our sons? Many of us would move heaven and earth to create opportunities for our children. We network, we call in favors, and we show up for those we love. So why is it different for LeBron? The current narrative says Bronny isn't NBA ready—but let's step back and ask: Ready by whose standards? And is readiness only defined by stats or draft pick numbers? Let's take a closer look.

Bronny has been around his dad his entire life—watching him in the gym, on the sidelines, attending practices, and soaking in years of elite preparation. Why is it suddenly a problem if someone makes a phone call and says, "Hey, my child, relative, or friend is looking for an opportunity"? That's not nepotism, that's networking. And in nearly every profession, we call that smart.

Maybe—just maybe—I can't prove this, but allow me to imagine it, not just as an author, but as a father. Perhaps Bronny was once asked at school during one of those "What do you want to be?" exercises. Many of us have answered that question by pointing to someone we admire in our own family. Maybe, just maybe, LeBron once wondered, "Is he really interested in this path?" Because LeBron knows what comes with it—the criticism, the media scrutiny, the pressure to perform.

Imagine Bronny, sitting courtside at one of his dad's championship games, hearing the crowd roar and the opposing fans boo. He may have thought to himself, "Could I handle that?" Or maybe something else sparked inside him—the determination to push through, the dream to be on the court, to earn a championship of his own. Maybe he didn't say it out loud, but quietly decided, "Yeah, I want this. I'm going to work for it."

Now, you might say, "But Darryll, this is different. The top media and professional analyst are saying Bronny isn't ready. There are way better players out there. He was picked 55th overall. If he was that good, he would've gone earlier."

To that, I say: if the NBA only cared about early round picks, they wouldn't have a 55th pick at all. To the analysts obsessed with saying Bronny isn't ready—go back and look at your own early years in the industry. I'm sure there were moments when people doubted you, just like you may have doubted someone else. Yet here you are. How many people have you proven wrong? Why not offer Bronny that same chance?

To the players who question his readiness—go back and watch your own rookie tape. Maybe you were only recruited for your defense or because of one standout skill. Not everyone walks into the league as a complete package. Remember, no one was shooting the three-ball at a high level until Stephen Curry redefined it. Unlike legends like Ray Allen, Reggie Miller, or even Larry Bird, Steph had to find a unique edge because of his smaller size. He did that by putting in countless hours of intentional work.

Yes, people actually get paid to tell you what you're not good at, or what you shouldn't be doing. But truth doesn't need validation from ignorance. Have we forgotten that Michael Jordan's high school coach once told him he wasn't good enough to make the team? Yet today, he's widely known as the GOAT—not just because of his stats, but because of his relentless will to win. Jordan consistently tapped into that inner drive we all have—the determination to push through opposition and the hunger to improve. Remember when he couldn't get past the Detroit Pistons? Instead of giving up, he spent the summer in the gym, building strength, and eventually overcame them. That's what growth looks like.

As a carpenter and a 51-year-old man, I submit to you that Bronny James is **work ready**. That's an attribute he's observed firsthand from his father throughout his life. Bronny knows how to work on his weaknesses and be honest about what those weaknesses are. He has one of the greatest of all time as a mentor. How many of us can say we had that? Not necessarily LeBron James, but someone who invested in us for the sake of our betterment—with no price tag, just love and guidance.

Then there is my story as a carpenter. I don't tell it often—not because I'm making excuses, but because I'm not about starting with sympathy. This is just the truth, and where I can't prove something, I'll let you know.

When I first started attending trade school, I faced enormous challenges. Eventually, I joined the union to advance my career, and on my very first job, I met a gentleman named Joe Caly, who later became a good friend. Joe told me, just hours into my career, "You better go back to school."

Challenge after challenge followed—maybe due to my race, or maybe because I hadn't yet developed the necessary skills. I entered this trade without any family background in construction, no legacy to follow, no one to lean on for guidance. But what I did have was work ethic. My grandfather instilled in me a deep sense of pride and an unwavering determination—not just to be good, but to be the best version of myself. Just like Bronny in his journey, we are all working and striving in our own lanes. Whether you realize it or not, someone is always watching—making sure you show up, give your best, and execute with excellence.

I was laid off with a pink slip marked "lack of work" on a site that clearly had more work to be done. But then there was Junior Hart, who encouraged me to stay the course. There was a moment when I wanted to quit altogether, and my grandfather told me, "Don't be a quitter. Keep going until you can't take anymore—then dig deep, because there's more in you." He said, "All you need is for someone to take you under their wing. keep working hard and learn all you can."

That moment came when I walked into the old Sears building in downtown Bridgeport to work on Housatonic Community College. The foreman Todd asked me, "Are you an apprentice or journeyman?" I told him I was a third-year apprentice. Todd began to ask me if I knew how to work with metal, Before I could respond further, I heard a voice say, "Yeah, he knows metal." It was a white guy named Guy Murray. Guy and I had never met before that day, and I wasn't sent there to meet up with him.

From that day forward, Guy said, "I'm going to teach you everything I know." He couldn't drive at the time and only worked jobs close to home. Despite missing a few fingers, a notable challenge in a hands-on profession—he still performed at a high level. He asked if I could pick him up for work, and since he lived just a few miles away, it worked out perfectly.

He became that mentor my grandfather spoke of—the one who would guide me. Had I quit, I would've missed that opportunity. Guy used to tell me, "What I'm teaching you will feed your family for the rest of your life." And he was right. What I learned from him went beyond carpentry. It taught me confidence and resilience. Over time, I was promoted to foreman. I worked under a man named Gary Vontell, known for firing people within hours. But through Guy's teaching, my family's encouragement, and my own work ethic, I held my own.

Gary once asked me, "Can you read blueprints?" I told him, "Yes." Reading blueprints is like learning to shoot a 3-pointer—it's a skill not everyone has. I took a set of prints home one day, as Guy suggested, and taught myself how to read them. That skill, like Bronny's basketball IQ, elevated me to the next level.

I was good with my hands—that came naturally. However interpreting blueprints required another level of understanding. Just like Bronny is working on his game from different spots on the court late nights and early mornings, I had to teach myself through long nights of study.

You may not have a father who can get you into the league or your dream job—but that's a false narrative anyway. What matters is hard work. Be patient, like I had to be until I met Guy.

I remember during my apprentice—or rookie—days—it felt like all I did was sweep. It was frustrating, especially after spending a year in school learning a trade that didn't include pushing a broom. One day, while sweeping a room where Terry McKnight was installing a ceiling, he turned to me and said, "How you doing, young fella?" I answered, "Man, this is Bull Shit, I'm just sweeping." Terry smiled and said, "You're not just sweeping. You're watching me install this ceiling. You're learning the materials, the process, and how things go together. You're preparing."

That stuck with me. Just like Bronny, whether sitting on the bench or watching from the sideline—he's studying. He's learning how players move, how plays are called, how the game flows in real time. That's part of the process. Even when you're not in the spotlight, you're still getting ready for your moment.

That moment stuck with me. Terry was right. A few weeks later, one of the guys went on vacation, and I was finally asked to put the broom down and strap on my tool belt. It was the opportunity I had been waiting for—and I was ready. That was over 30 years ago, and I still remember it like it was yesterday.

Bronny will one day look back on this season of his life, too. Maybe you've had moments where you've had to stay ready and be patient. If not, keep living, You will. Let people encourage you. Stay open to unexpected mentors. Be teachable, Be coachable, sometimes, that's all you need.

Yes, I declare that Bronny is ready—not just for the NBA, but for whatever comes next. Work ethic isn't something everyone has. Height, skill, and natural ability might open doors, but it's discipline and effort that keep those doors open. Take Muggsy Bogues, for example one of the shortest players to ever step onto an NBA court. He wasn't the tallest, strongest, or flashiest, but he worked hard. He recognized his limitations and mastered his advantages. Muggsy was the shortest player on the court—not occasionally, but **every single game**—and still made a lasting impact through grit and perseverance.

Bronny is work-ready. He will continue to improve and grow because he's **developed the habit**. And for those of you reading this who feel like you didn't get off to a good start, or that life didn't deal you a fair hand—get back in the lab. Keep working. Greatness may never come with public applause. You might not make the Hall of Fame. You might not get the acknowledgment. You might get the Bronny treatment—where everyone's talking but few are watching the work.

All of that is okay, just remember: **the work you put in is what makes you ready** for **whatever** it is you decide to pursue, no one gets to validate that but you.

VICTORY, NOT VIOLENCE

Violence is often mistaken for strength. Across cultures, generations, and backgrounds, men have been conditioned to believe that power is asserted through force—that to be victorious, one must dominate. The battlefield of masculinity has been waged in schoolyards, bar fights, and even boardrooms, where respect is seen as something to be earned through aggression rather than intellect, emotional intelligence, or restraint. But what if victory had nothing to do with violence? What if true strength lay not in the ability to harm, but in the discipline to walk away?

Respect—or the lack of it—is at the core of male violence. A single moment of perceived disrespect can escalate into a fight, a shooting, or a war. From young boys to grown men, the instinct to respond to disrespect with aggression is deeply ingrained. It's a reflex, an expectation, a social script passed down through generations. The idea that a man must "handle" his problems with his fists or through revenge is not just an individual flaw—it's a cultural conditioning.

But violence doesn't come from nowhere. It is learned, reinforced, and rewarded. We see it in the media we consume, in the games we play, in the way we are taught to resolve conflict. The modern world has created a disconnect from death, from consequence, from the reality of harm. In video games, players kill and respawn. In movies, heroes settle scores through bloodshed and are glorified for doing so. In social settings, men who back down are labeled weak. The message is clear: to be respected, one must be feared.

At the same time, anger is an emotion that men are allowed to express freely, while vulnerability is discouraged. Boys are taught early on to "man up" and suppress their feelings—except when it comes to rage. This anger, left unchecked and without alternative outlets, turns into aggression. A young boy pushed to the edge doesn't cry; he punches a hole in the wall. A man humiliated in front of his peers doesn't talk it out; he seeks revenge.

And then, there's the body as a weapon. Many men don't just train their bodies for health or appearance, but for combat—consciously or unconsciously preparing for a moment when they must prove themselves through violence. Muscles become armor, fists become tools of enforcement. The gym, once a place for self-improvement, can become a forge for battle-readiness. Not for sport, but for survival in a world where conflict is always lurking.

But what if there was another way? What if respect wasn't something that had to be beaten into others, but something that was commanded through wisdom, leadership, and self-control? What if true victory wasn't about conquering another man, but conquering one's own impulses?

The fight isn't against another person; it's against the expectation that violence is the only answer.

The Draw to Gangs: A False Promise of Brotherhood and Power

For many young men, joining a gang is not just about crime—it is about survival, identity, and belonging. The streets become a home, and the gang becomes a family in places where traditional support structures have failed. Poverty, absent fathers, and lack of mentorship leave a void, and gangs fill it with a sense of purpose, protection, and respect.

Men are drawn to gangs despite knowing the risks—jail, violence, and even death—because they often feel they have no alternative. In environments where jobs are scarce, schools are underfunded, and role models are absent, the gang lifestyle offers something that many young men desperately crave: respect. Respect, however, comes at a cost. The same loyalty that brings them in often forces them to commit acts of violence, perpetuating a cycle they cannot easily escape.

Gangs also provide a sense of masculinity that many young men feel they must uphold. The idea of dominance, revenge, and never backing down is deeply embedded in gang culture, mirroring the same societal scripts that equate manhood with aggression. When violence becomes a rite of passage, it ceases to be a choice and instead becomes an expectation. Oftentimes, a criminal act is part of the initiation process. I encourage those thinking about it to look at the lives of previous individuals; most of them want to deter you from getting involved with a gang.

Breaking the Cycle: Prevention and Intervention

To slow the outcry of young men being drawn into this way of life, the community must provide alternatives that are just as compelling as the gangs themselves. Society is a larger space often you are not included or come to understand what societal norms are. Community is up close and interactive with you and your family. When you communicate or come together, this can be effective. There used to be a time when, as a collective, even in the worst neighborhoods, people would come together in the community to get involved to help our youth. Businesses, churches, and all other organizations have to come together and look for ways to prevent violence and disagreement with alternative solutions. The way kids have access to weapons these days, and the short amount of time it takes for a situation to escalate to a person losing their life. The way a teenager or young adult can go from a future looking bright to getting caught by a stray bullet. the way a child just in his or her stroller being pushed through the mall can suffer injuries because of a mass shooting. Programs like *Scared Straight* once aimed to deter at-risk youth by exposing them to the harsh realities of prison life. While these programs had some impact, they did not address the deeper, systemic issues that push young men toward gangs and violence in the first place.

Effective intervention requires a multi-faceted approach:

1. **Mentorship and Role Models** – Young men need positive influences who can guide them toward constructive paths. Community leaders, former gang members, and responsible men who have walked the same streets can provide the mentorship that is often lacking at home.

2. **Education and Economic Opportunities** – Providing access to quality education, vocational training, and employment opportunities can create alternatives to gang life. When young men see a viable future outside of crime, they are less likely to engage in it.

3. **Conflict Resolution Training** – Teaching emotional intelligence and alternative ways to handle conflict can help break the cycle of violence. Programs in schools, community centers, and juvenile facilities can equip young

men with the skills to de-escalate situations without resorting to aggression.

4. **Reintegration Programs for Former Gang Members** – Many young men who wish to leave the gang lifestyle fear retribution or have no clear exit strategy. Reintegration programs can provide support systems, job placement, and counseling to help them transition away from violence.

5. **Restorative Justice and Community Engagement** – Encouraging community-driven solutions where former gang members engage with youth to share their experiences and warn of the consequences can be a powerful deterrent. Creating spaces where young men feel valued and heard can prevent them from seeking validation through violence.

6. **Family and Strong Support SystemS**

One of the most powerful tools for keeping young men out of gangs and away from violence is a strong, consistent support system. Family doesn't have to mean perfect—it means present. A young man who knows someone is checking in on him, rooting for him, correcting him when needed, and simply showing up, stands a better chance at navigating life's challenges without turning to the streets.

Support starts at home, but it extends beyond the walls of the house. Uncles, grandfathers, cousins, stepfathers, mentors, and close family friends can all play a role. For many, the absence of a biological father is real, but that absence doesn't have to create a void if the community steps in to fill it. Male presence and consistent guidance give a young man a sense of accountability, identity, and direction.

When the home is unstable, chaotic, or neglectful, gangs can look like family. They offer loyalty, belonging, and protection—but at a dangerous cost. A strong support system at home makes it less likely that a young man will need to seek those things elsewhere. He needs to know he's not alone, even when he makes mistakes. He needs truth, correction, encouragement, and love—especially when he doesn't know how to ask for it.

Community centers, faith-based programs, and local organizations can also function as an extended family. These networks provide structure, purpose, and positive examples. When young men are surrounded by adults who invest in their growth, the streets lose their appeal.

Building a Future Without Violence

Eliminating violence requires not only intervention but also proactive strategies to create long-term change. Communities must invest in programs that promote emotional intelligence, accountability, and resilience from an early age. Schools should integrate conflict resolution and anger management into their curriculum, equipping young men with the tools they need to navigate adversity without resorting to aggression.

Creating safe spaces where young men can openly discuss their emotions and experiences can help dismantle the stigma around vulnerability. Encouraging fathers, mentors, and male role models to exemplify nonviolent leadership will reinforce the message that strength lies in self-control, not in force.

Society must shift the cultural narrative away from glorifying violent behavior and instead celebrate those who lead with wisdom and integrity. By changing the perception of masculinity, empowering young men with positive alternatives, and fostering a community-centered approach, we can move toward a future where victory is measured not by dominance but by the ability to uplift and inspire others.

MOMMAS BOY

I must admit, **being called a "momma's boy"** is a name no man wants to hear. If you do, it's likely in a heated moment—usually when someone isn't getting their way. While that's just one scenario, the label carries weight and meaning that's worth unpacking.

Let me be clear: I would never deny the love I have for my mother. But many children today are raised in single-parent households, with over 80% of them headed by single mothers, according to the 2021 Census. That's significant. It means, in many cases, the mother is not just the caregiver; she becomes the dominant role model.

This doesn't mean that in a two-parent household, a mother's love is less important. But when she's the only one there day in and day out, that bond might naturally become even stronger. Who else is the child supposed to turn to? In some cases, there are visitation arrangements, like the one I had with my son. It wasn't easy; I had to fight in court just to be part of his life.

As a child growing up, I remember my mom once referring to herself as both my mother and my father. Of course, that's not genetically possible, but the weight of raising two kids alone led her to say it—and I don't hold that against her. Still, every relationship needs boundaries, and that includes the one between a mother and her son.

On the surface, **"momma's boy"** might sound like just a joke or jab, but it's something that deserves an explanation if you're going to call me that. Like many men, I wouldn't take kindly to being labeled that way—once is more than enough. **Name-calling is never productive**, and in this case, it often feels like an attempt to create division between a mother and her child.

At the same time, a mother must understand her place in her son's life. She shouldn't overstep her role, especially if she already knows where the boundaries are. A mom should be patient, allowing her son to bring her into his world on his own terms—not by prying, snooping, or making assumptions. And guilt-tripping him for not being as available as he once was? That's not fair either.

Of course, if you can be there for your mom, you should be. And if you can't, you might still find ways to help, even from a distance. Everyone needs support sometimes, and I'd like to believe my own kids will be there for me when I'm no longer able to do everything myself.

It's often said that the way a man treats his mother is how he'll treat his partner. But that's not always true. Some men are scarred by their relationship with their mom and don't treat her well—but that doesn't mean they won't treat their partner with love and respect. Still, if there's damage in that bond, it's worth trying to heal it, especially if children are involved. After all, there's nothing like having grandparents in your child's life.

Personally, I've never been one to tell my mother negative things about my partner. The relationship between you and your mom and between you and your partner doesn't have to be complicated—**not if everyone has mutual respect** and a clear understanding of their roles.

Healthy disagreements are okay. As men, we're responsible for making sure both of these important relationships are strong and growing. When done right, everyone benefits.

Having a wife or partner doesn't mean your parents lose their role in your life. That bond still matters. And when people talk about being "evenly yoked," they often forget how important shared values are. If your partner has never had a strong relationship with her mom, she might not understand the value of that connection in your life.

In the end, being close to your mom doesn't make you a "momma's boy" in the negative sense. It makes you human. The key is balance, respect, and boundaries—because when those are in place, love has the space to thrive.

DEALING WITH LOSSES

Loss is an inevitable part of life. Whether it's the loss of a loved one, a relationship, a job, money, or even something as simple as a favorite sports team losing a big game, the feeling of loss can affect us in profound ways. From childhood to adulthood, we all learn how to deal with loss in different forms, and how we manage these moments can shape our character, resilience, and ability to move forward.

We all know how it goes—we have a team that has never made it to the Super Bowl, or maybe they finally do, and we are glued to the TV with the expectation of talking smack to someone rooting for the other team. The joy of celebrating a win and rubbing it in a rival's face is part of the fun, but ultimately, these types of losses are novelty and should be taken as such. We shouldn't lose sleep over them or let them affect our well-being.

Learning to Lose: The Early Lessons

As a kid, I learned how to deal with losses through sports. Growing up in Bridgeport, CT, playing baseball, kickball, and even video games, I experienced firsthand what it meant to win and lose. I vividly remember the first time my team lost a baseball game, and it became very clear to me that if I continued playing, I would have to deal with the feeling of not winning. It didn't feel good, especially when friends teased me about the loss, sometimes blaming me directly.

We were all close; we went to school together, lived in the same neighborhood, and winning was essential. I recall a game when I was pitching; I was the second or third best pitcher on the team, and we were facing the Twins, a very good team. Two outs, two men on base, and I was pitching to Tweetie, a tall guy who crowded the plate and could hit anything over it out of the park. My good friend Roddy came to the mound, took the ball, then took my hand and placed it on the ball. He said, "Harmon, this is a curveball. Throw this pitch as hard as you can." I did just that and got Tweety out. The fear of losing, the fear of him sending my fastball over the cones, was enough for me. We don't always have control over our wins and losses—sometimes, all we can do is face the loss and move forward.

Then came video games, where losing was even more personal. There was no team to hide behind—just me and my opponent. Sometimes it was my cousin, my friends, but losing in a one-on-one competition that felt different. But over time, I learned something: loss was part of the game, part of growth. Losing pushed me to practice harder, to study the game, and to become better. Some people equate losing with failing, but I see loss as a teacher—painful, yes, but also necessary for progress.

LeBron James

One of the most recognized basketball players in NBA history, LeBron James, is arguably the greatest of all time. He became the NBA's all-time leading scorer, surpassing Kareem Abdul-Jabbar's 38,387 points on February 7, 2023, a date I remember clearly because it was just a day before my grandmother's 97th birthday.

The moment was bittersweet, as she had passed away two days prior.

LeBron has seemingly defied Father Time, still competing at an MVP level in his 22nd season, tying Vince Carter for longevity. Over his career, he has won championships with three different teams: bringing a title to his hometown of Cleveland with the Cavaliers, winning two in Miami alongside Hall of Famer Dwyane Wade, and securing another with one of the most historic and recognized sports franchises in the world, the Los Angeles Lakers, where he continues to play.

LeBron's legacy extends beyond the court, as he has two sons who also play basketball. His oldest, Bronny James, was recently drafted by the Lakers, setting the stage for a historic moment: the first father-son duo to play together in the NBA.

Then there's his finals record—eight straight Finals appearances, ten in total, but only four championships to show for it. Many enjoy comparing him to Michael Jordan, sparking debates about who the true GOAT is. However, rather than focus on the number of championships or Finals losses, I prefer to look at LeBron's mindset, preparation, and focus. Over two decades, through 82-game seasons (even when injuries sidelined him at times), he remained determined, never allowing setbacks to define him. He moved on, always prepared to win again.

The sacrifices he has made, the challenges he has faced—through his normal life, the things people have said about him on and off social media on major sports networks, and the pressures of being a global icon, all speak to his perseverance. I salute LeBron James. To me, the GOAT debate isn't necessary, and it shouldn't revolve around Finals losses. No matter what side of the debate people are on, his greatness is undeniable.

Losing People: The Reality of Life

As I got older, I realized that loss extended far beyond games and competition. Losing people—whether to death, distance, or broken relationships—was a different kind of pain, one that no amount of practice could prepare me for.

The first real loss I experienced was the passing of my friend Chantelle "Reesie" Gray. We grew up together in PT Barnum apartments—walking to school, laughing, joking, just living life. And then, one day, he was gone. I remember getting the news that he had been gunned down and found dead on a porch in the morning.

The ironic thing was, I had unknowingly walked past his body, covered in a white sheet, that same morning. When I got to school, another good friend mentioned that something had happened the night before and that no one knew where Reesie was. It was only then that I realized the body I had seen was his.

This wasn't like a baseball game where I could get another chance. There was no reset button like in a video game. There would be no do-over, no opportunity to say what I wish I had said, to make things right, or to relive those moments.

During that time, there were so many losses—too many to name. I recall becoming numb to it all, deciding at one point that I wouldn't attend any more funerals. My mother would often ask, "Did you know that guy?" and all I could do was nod. It was a dark time, but even then, nothing prepared me for the depth of loss I felt when I lost my grandfather.

That loss taught me that some things in life are final. It forced me to appreciate the people around me while they were still here and to be mindful of the words left unsaid. The pain of losing someone isn't just about their absence; it's about the memories you wish you could make of them and the words you never got to say. I'm a different individual now than I was then. Oh, how our conversations would be now. He was such a wise man, 86 when he left this earth, such a blessing to be able to say goodbye to a loved one.

On the other hand, when my dad passed, it was unexpected. I knew he had some medical issues, and I was actually preparing to have him move in with me. Pops called me while I was on vacation in Florida, and I told him I would come by as soon as I got back. I visited him on Monday, and he told me the doctor had informed him that his cancer had returned. Knowing all he had been through and the changes he was making, I asked him if he was getting tired. He assured me he was not.

Just two days later, I got a call that he was being rushed to the hospital as he was unresponsive. I rushed to where he was just as he was being put into an ambulance. I followed behind, running every red light, risking being stopped by the police. When we arrived at the hospital, it was surreal. The nurses asked me what I wanted to do—he had a Do Not Resuscitate order, and he was not breathing on his own. With no time to think, I decided to honor the order.

To my surprise, my dad didn't pass at that moment. As the day went on, I asked question after question, trying to understand what had happened. The doctors told me he had life-ending cancer and needed to be placed in hospice care. I agreed, thinking this was the best way to keep him comfortable. At this point, he was alert but unable to speak, and he had swelling on his upper lip, possibly from a fall.

As the night grew long, I continued to question the medical staff about his condition. They rejected my suggestions to move him or update his medical records, insisting that he wouldn't make it through the next few hours. However, well into the next morning, August 29th, a nurse came in and asked what had happened. After I explained, she told me his vitals were good and suggested taking him off hospice so he could receive medication. The night nurse, responding to my request, confirmed that he was stable and said they would grant my request when the doctor came in around 7 a.m.

Thinking he was improving, I decided to go home, shower, and change. As I lay down for a quick nap, I received a call around 6 a.m. saying my dad had passed.

After a couple of weeks of this not sitting well with me, I called his doctor, the one he was supposed to see the week he died. The doctor had no idea my dad had passed. I asked him what he was going to tell my dad, and his response was, "He had about a year or two to live." This still remains a mystery to me.

By this time, I had grown to understand death, especially the loss of close loved ones. Even weeks after my dad's passing, I would instinctively pick up the phone to call him—only to realize he was gone. With my grandmother and mother still alive, I knew I needed to prepare better, so I started recording sit-down conversations with them. Then, that moment came. I got the call that my Nana had passed. You see, I no longer live in the same state, and for anyone who has lost a loved one from a distance, the feeling is uniquely difficult. As I prepared for it, I lay in my bed watching the recorded conversations that I had prepared for this moment. This was my way of dealing with this loss. My nana and I were close, and I owe so much to her, and I celebrate her every day.

Divorce: A Different Kind of Loss

Divorce is a unique type of loss that often carries emotional, financial, and psychological consequences. Unlike other losses, it can be a long, drawn-out process that affects not just the two people separating but also children, family, and even close friends. For men, dealing with divorce can be particularly challenging, as society often expects them to suppress emotions and simply move on. However, the reality is that divorce can create feelings of failure, regret, and uncertainty about the future.

Let me be clear—I don't advocate divorce. I advocate recovery. Sometimes life doesn't go the way we planned, but regardless of the loss, **life does go on**. Don't beat yourself up. Own what you may have done—or didn't do—that contributed to the situation and then move on quickly. You don't want to find yourself stuck in a pity party, replaying what you lost or how much time you think you wasted. Instead, reflect on what you've learned from it all. Every ending carries a lesson, and how you respond determines your growth.

As discussed earlier in this chapter, every form of separation requires healing—and divorce is no different. It's not just the end of a relationship; it's the end of a shared routine, a sense of belonging, and sometimes even identity. When the home becomes divided, the emotional weight can feel heavier than expected, especially when you're still trying to keep it together for everyone else.

One of the hardest parts of divorce is when children are involved. The dynamic of fatherhood changes, and many men find themselves fighting for time with their kids. Custody battles, child support, and co-parenting struggles can add layers of stress that linger long after the relationship ends. Some men experience the pain of feeling like a visitor in their child's life, while others must work to rebuild trust with their children, who may not understand why the family structure changed.

As we discussed in *Self-Preservation*, protecting your emotional and mental well-being is critical. That same principle applies here. Men need to process the emotional impact of divorce rather than burying it under work, distractions, or unhealthy habits. Pain that is ignored doesn't disappear, it multiplies. Finding support, whether through therapy, as I did, through faith, or through trusted friends—can make all the difference in navigating this major life change.

Divorce does not have to define a man, but how he handles it will shape his future and the relationships he builds moving forward. Use it as an opportunity to grow—to rediscover yourself, reassess your priorities, and learn how to love again without losing yourself in the process.

Some men delay the inevitable out of fear of being alone. But staying in a situation that drains your peace is no victory either. Whatever your reason for staying or leaving, take time to process this loss properly. Divorce can feel as significant as the loss of a loved one, and it deserves the same level of healing and reflection. You can rebuild—but first, you must allow yourself to break, acknowledge the pain, and then rise from it stronger, wiser, and more aware of what truly matters.

Loss of Friendships

Friendship can be one of the strongest bonds in a person's life, yet they are not immune to loss. Unlike family, friendships are chosen, and when they end, they can leave a void just as painful as losing a loved one. Friendships can be lost for many reasons—misunderstandings, feelings of being undervalued, or differences in life progression. One person may achieve success or reach new milestones while the other feels left behind. Sometimes, the bond fades because of choices; perhaps a friend becomes close to someone you don't get along with, creating tension that neither side wants to address.

What makes the loss of a friendship even harder is that, in many cases, it is preventable. People often speak about bridges being broken, but I believe a bridge isn't truly broken until you refuse to pay the toll of communication to get over it. Too many friendships end due to unspoken frustrations and misinterpretations that, if discussed openly, could be resolved.

The key to navigating the loss of a friendship is to reflect on whether the relationship is truly over or if it's simply going through a difficult phase. If the friendship was genuine, a conversation—no matter how uncomfortable—could be all it takes to rebuild the bond. But if both parties refuse to communicate, the bridge remains closed, and the friendship becomes just another loss to be accepted. Knowing when to fight for a friendship and when to let go with grace is a skill that requires maturity, self-awareness, and humility.

Other Types of Loss

Loss comes in many forms, and while some are replaceable, others are not. I break them down into three main categories:

1. **Loss of Material Things** – This includes losing personal belongings, money, or even a home. While frustrating and sometimes devastating, material losses can often be recovered over time.

2. **Loss of Opportunities** – Losing a job, missing out on a promotion, or even failing to capitalize on a once-in-a-lifetime chance can be hard to process. These losses can make us question our worth, but they can also serve as motivation to prepare for the next opportunity.

In the Still of the Night

Certain life situations keep people awake at night—divorce, job loss, financial struggles, grief, or uncertainty about the future. When the phone stops ringing and messages stop coming, the silence can feel overwhelming. Many turn to distractions like endless social media scrolling, hoping for relief. But what do you do when that no longer works?

Some look to alcohol or substances to self-medicate, while others rely on herbal teas or natural supplements to help them sleep. In some cases, a professional evaluation may be necessary to determine whether underlying issues like anxiety or insomnia are at play. Another factor could be a medical diagnosis. Chronic pain, hormonal imbalances, or neurological conditions can disrupt sleep patterns, making it difficult to rest even when exhaustion sets in. If sleep disturbances persist, consulting a doctor can help identify whether an underlying health issue is contributing to the problem.

Racing thoughts can make rest feel impossible, and turning off external noise—like the TV—can sometimes help. The key is understanding whether it's just the situation keeping you up or something deeper.

Nighttime is often when unresolved emotions surface. During the day, we stay busy working, handling responsibilities, and engaging with others. But at night, when everything slows down, suppressed thoughts begin to take over. This is why so many struggle with sleep; the weight of regrets, present worries, and future uncertainties can feel unbearable.

Sleepless nights can create a cycle of overthinking and anxiety. Some replay past conversations, dwell on mistakes, or stress about the unknown. If you struggle to find rest, developing a nighttime routine can help quiet your mind. Journaling, practicing deep breathing, or listening to calming music can promote relaxation.

Many also turn to unhealthy habits to cope. Late-night overeating, excessive drinking, or substance use may provide temporary relief but often lead to greater problems. Instead of seeking quick fixes, it's essential to address the root cause of what keeps you up.

Talking about your thoughts can be a powerful way to find relief. If you have a trusted friend, mentor, or family member, sharing your feelings can lighten the emotional burden. If opening up feels too difficult, seeking professional help might be the best step. Therapy is now more accessible than ever, with online options allowing people to connect with licensed counselors from home.

For some, spirituality provides comfort. Prayer, meditation, or practicing gratitude can shift the focus from stress to peace. Others find solace in writing letters to themselves, using the process as a way to acknowledge and release emotions.

If you're like me, you may wake up in the middle of the night before a big event the next day. One of the hardest parts of writing for me is maintaining good sleep—I often find myself waking at odd hours, needing to grab a pen and paper to clear my mind. Recognizing these patterns and finding ways to manage them is key.

Lack of sleep not only affects mental well-being but also has significant physical consequences. Chronic sleep deprivation weakens the immune system, increases the risk of heart disease, and impacts brain function. People who consistently get poor sleep struggle with focus, decision-making, and emotional regulation. Over time, exhaustion leads to burnout, making it even harder to handle life's challenges.

If you frequently find yourself lying awake, ask what unresolved issues may be causing it. Are you holding onto anger, guilt, or fear? Are you stressing over things outside of your control? Sometimes, acknowledging these feelings is the first step toward finding peace.

Creating a bedtime routine that encourages relaxation can make a significant difference. Avoiding screens before bed, drinking herbal tea, reading, or practicing mindfulness can help signal to your brain that it's time to rest. Making your bedroom a peaceful space—free from clutter and distractions—can also improve sleep quality.

Ultimately, the goal is to confront what keeps you awake rather than allowing it to linger. Ignoring emotional struggles only prolongs the pain and makes it harder to function. Whether through self-reflection, healthy coping mechanisms, or professional support, taking control of your mental and emotional well-being leads to healing and, eventually, restful nights.

Don't hesitate to seek professional help. Therapy and counseling are more available than ever, making it easier to connect with professionals. Many of us struggle to process difficult situations, and when left unaddressed, they can spiral out of control. Managing stress and emotional turmoil proactively is key to maintaining long-term mental health.

Handling Loss with Strength and Perspective

No matter the type of loss, how we handle it determines how we move forward. When I lost my grandfather, I knew it was coming age had slowed him down, and reality told me that his time was near. But knowing that loss is coming doesn't always make it easier to process. It's still painful, still leaves a void, and still forces reflection.

Through every loss I've faced, one thing has remained true: if I give 100% of myself with good intentions, the outcome—whether a win or a loss—is easier to accept. When I practiced hard in baseball, even if I lost, I knew I had done everything I could. When I invested time in my relationships, even if they didn't work out, I could walk away knowing I had given my best. And in the event, you reflect and find correction, that's just as fine—**apologize if you can and learn from it.** Move on with maturity and emotional control, knowing that self-awareness is a form of strength, not shame.

Always allow yourself to feel how you feel—**without judgment.** Don't rush it, and don't try to busy yourself through it. Grief, disappointment, and change are all part of the human experience. The sooner you embrace how you feel, the sooner you can heal. Pressure lives all around us, and loss only adds more of it. If you don't give yourself time to release it, that pressure will find its own way out—and not always in healthy forms.

Loss is inevitable, but regret is avoidable.

We can't escape loss, but we can choose how we respond to it. As I mentioned in *Self-Preservation*, awareness and balance are key.

Whether through resilience, faith, forgiveness, or finding a new purpose, dealing with losses is about learning, growing, and continuing forward despite setbacks.

The question isn't whether you will experience loss, it's how you will handle it when it comes.

When that moment does arrive, meet it with reflection, not reaction. Learn from it, recover from it, and remind yourself that you're still here for a reason. Every loss, when faced with strength and perspective, becomes a stepping-stone toward wisdom and peace.

ADDICTIONS AND DISTRACTIONS

Addictions and distractions that come in forms—some are obvious, while others are more subtle but equally damaging. Whether it's substance abuse, technology, workaholism, or unhealthy behavioral patterns, these habits shape our lives and impact our homes, communities, health, and finances. Understanding their effects and learning how to break free from their grip is crucial to becoming the best version of ourselves.

The Nature of Addiction

Addiction is more than just dependence on a substance; it is a compulsive behavior that overrides logic, priorities, and self-control. Substance abuse, gambling, overeating, and even excessive gaming or social media use can hijack our lives, leading to devastating consequences. Many of these behaviors start as a means of coping—escaping stress, trauma, or pain—but over time, they become prisons that are hard to escape.

Some people are emotional eaters, turning to food, especially sweets, as a way to cope with stress, sadness, or anxiety. This can lead to excessive sugar intake, weight gain, and long-term health issues such as diabetes. Instead of allowing the addiction to control you, deal with the underlying emotions that cause it. If you are an emotional eater, ask yourself—what emotion drives you to eat? Many people eat in response to sadness rather than hunger, using food as a temporary comfort rather than addressing the root cause of their distress. Similarly, others engage in emotional shopping, buying things impulsively to fill an emotional void. Have you ever heard someone say, "I need a drink" when going through a stressful situation? This kind of coping mechanism can evolve into dependency, reinforcing destructive cycles of behavior rather than addressing the root cause of the stress.

Nicotine and vaping have also become common ways to deal with stress. Many people turn to cigarettes or vape pens as a quick way to calm anxiety or tension. However, these habits can quickly turn into addictions that negatively impact lung health, cardiovascular function, and overall well-being. Rather than relying on nicotine to manage stress, individuals should explore healthier alternatives like deep breathing exercises, meditation, physical activity, or talking to a trusted friend or therapist.

My grandmother once told me she had a shoe addiction because, growing up, she had to share her shoes with her mother. When she was finally able to afford her own, she overcompensated by buying more than she needed. This story was important for me to hear because it showed how past deprivation can lead to overindulgence. This principle applies to many areas of life—when we lack something growing up, we often seek to overcorrect once we have control over it. However, moderation is key.

People have many types of addictions beyond the obvious. Gambling, for instance, has become more accessible than ever with online sports betting, leading many into financial ruin. The thrill of winning can quickly become a destructive cycle of debt and loss. Other addictions, like excessive shopping, may seem harmless but can lead to financial instability and compulsive behavior. Sex addiction and pornography consumption are also often overlooked, yet they can deeply impact relationships and even marriages. In some cases, such addictions are rooted in deeper trauma, such as molestation or early exposure to unhealthy sexual behaviors, which can shape one's perception of intimacy in damaging ways.

The Crack Baby Era and Its Lasting Effects

One of the most overlooked aspects of addiction's generational impact is the legacy of the crack epidemic. During the 1980s and 1990s, thousands of children were born to mothers who used crack cocaine during pregnancy. These so-called "crack babies" faced numerous challenges, from developmental delays to social stigma. While not all were born with physical dependencies, many were raised in unstable environments where addiction, poverty, and neglect were common.

Today, the effects of that era linger. Many who were born during that time may not be addicted to drugs themselves but are more susceptible to substance abuse, risky behaviors, and struggles with impulse control. The trauma of growing up in environments shaped by addiction can manifest in several ways, from emotional instability to difficulties in relationships.

In today's world, new drugs have taken the place of crack cocaine, bringing their own devastating consequences. Marijuana, opioids, fentanyl, and other synthetic drugs have created a new wave of addiction that affects not just individuals but entire communities. The accessibility and normalization of these substances, particularly among younger generations, make the issue even more complex. Fentanyl, in particular, has led to an increase in fatal overdoses, as even small amounts can be deadly. The opioid crisis has devastated families, leaving children to grow up without parents and perpetuating cycles of trauma and instability.

If you are using drugs and planning to have a child, I encourage you to stop during the conception phase. Give the child a chance to be as healthy as they possibly can. Substance use during pregnancy can have lasting effects that go beyond birth, shaping a child's physical and mental development for years to come.

Addictions and Distractions

Addictions and distractions come in many forms—some are obvious, while others are more subtle but equally damaging. Whether it's substance abuse, technology, workaholism, or unhealthy behavioral patterns, these habits shape our lives and impact our homes, communities, health, and finances. Understanding their effects and learning how to break free from their grip is crucial to becoming the best version of ourselves.

The Power of Distractions

Not all distractions are inherently bad. Entertainment, social media, and hobbies can provide relaxation and mental relief. However, when distractions become avoidance mechanisms, they hinder growth. Many men bury themselves in their phones, sports, or work to escape personal struggles, often spending entire Sundays watching games without balance, failing to address the deeper issues at hand. The key is recognizing when a distraction has turned into a barrier to progress.

Social media platforms like TikTok, Facebook, and Instagram have become some of the biggest distractions of modern times. While they can be tools for networking and entertainment, they also create a false sense of reality, encouraging people to compare their lives to curated online images. Scrolling endlessly through content can lead to wasted hours, reduced productivity, and a decline in meaningful face-to-face interactions. These platforms are designed to keep users engaged, often leading to addiction-like behaviors where people struggle to put their phones down, even in moments that require their full attention.

Gaming is one of the most consuming distractions for many men. As video games have developed over the years, their realism and immersive nature have intensified, making it easy to spend hours lost in virtual worlds. While gaming can be a form of stress relief and entertainment, it can also develop into both a distraction and an addiction. Excessive gaming can lead to desensitization to reality, a lack of punctuality, and an absence of presence when it is most needed. Many men struggle to balance their responsibilities with gaming, leading to neglect in relationships, work, and personal development.

Workaholism is another form of distraction that can be mistaken for productivity. One of the things I had to balance was my work-life balance. I'm not sure if I was addicted to work as much as I was addicted to providing for my family. This imbalance prompted my mother to tell me one day, "All work and no play makes Jack a dull boy." If I have to be honest, although I've made progress and have slowed down as I've gotten older, this has always been a struggle for me. Now, I seem to be in a good place, but it took time and awareness to get here. Understanding that excessive work can be just as harmful as any other addiction is key to maintaining a well-rounded life. Not all distractions are inherently bad. Entertainment, social media, and hobbies can provide relaxation and mental relief. However, when distractions become avoidance mechanisms, they hinder growth. Many men bury themselves in their phones, TV shows, or work to escape personal struggles, failing to address the deeper issues at hand. The key is recognizing when a distraction has turned into a barrier to progress.

Social media platforms like TikTok, Facebook, and Instagram have become some of the biggest distractions of modern times. While they can be tools for networking and entertainment, they also create a false sense of reality, encouraging people to compare their lives to curated online images. Scrolling endlessly through content can lead to wasted hours, reduced productivity, and a decline in meaningful face-to-face interactions. These platforms are designed to keep users engaged, often leading to addiction-like behaviors where people struggle to put their phones down, even in moments that require their full attention.

Gaming is one of the most consuming distractions for many men. As video games have developed over the years, their realism and immersive nature have intensified, making it easy to spend hours lost in virtual worlds. While gaming can be a form of stress relief and entertainment, it can also develop into both a distraction and an addiction. Excessive gaming can lead to desensitization to reality, a lack of punctuality, and an absence of presence when it is most needed. Many men struggle to balance their responsibilities with gaming, leading to neglect in relationships, work, and personal development.

Before Amazon, there was the Shopping Network platform that made it easy to buy products with the simple press of a button. I recall a friend at work who was a smoker. His wife had purchased a cigarette roller through the Shopping Network, and as he told me the story, he also revealed a deeper issue—it wasn't just the cigarette roller, but his wife had become addicted to shopping and ordering things online. Today, we see the same addiction with Amazon and other online retailers. The ease and convenience of ordering right from your cell phone has made impulsive shopping more prevalent than ever.

Just like the introduction of debit cards increased spending by removing the tangible act of handling cash, online shopping fuels addictive behaviors. There was a time when people would pause to count the money in their pockets before making a purchase. Nowadays, many don't even know how much is in their bank account—they simply swipe, click, and spend without second thought. This lack of financial awareness can lead to overspending, financial instability, and an overall unhealthy relationship with money.

Impact on Home and Family

Addictions and distractions don't just affect the individual; they ripple through the home. A father who is always working may provide financially but lacks emotional presence. A husband addicted to social media may neglect real-life conversations with his spouse. Substance abuse can break families apart, eroding trust and stability. Recognizing these patterns is essential to maintaining a strong and healthy household.

The change in your behavior can be transferred to your children, often causing them to become stressed from the high-tension atmosphere they seem to constantly be in. A stress-free environment is crucial for children to grow up in, as it fosters emotional stability, confidence, and the ability to develop healthy relationships. When a home is filled with anxiety and tension due to addiction or unchecked distractions, children absorb that energy, which can affect their mental well-being and future decision-making. Addictions and distractions don't just affect the individual; they ripple through the home. A father who is always working may provide financially but lacks emotional presence. A husband addicted to social media may neglect real-life conversations with his spouse. Substance abuse can break families apart, eroding trust and stability. Recognizing these patterns is essential to maintaining a strong and healthy household.

The Community Effect

What happens at home spills into the community. A society filled with distracted and addicted individuals struggles to progress. The condition of our neighborhoods often mirrors the condition of the people within them. When homes are unstable, hearts become hardened, and communities begin to fracture.

Crime, poverty, and broken relationships often have roots in unchecked addictions and emotional neglect. When men lose focus, the ripple effect is felt everywhere—on the streets, in schools, and inside households. In *Victory, Not Violence*, I spoke about awareness and respect; those same principles apply here. A lack of awareness and respect for self eventually turns into a lack of respect for others.

Communities thrive when individuals are engaged, present, and intentional about their growth. One man choosing recovery can influence a household. One household choosing structure can influence a block. One block choosing accountability can influence a neighborhood. Real change doesn't start at city hall—it starts in living rooms, kitchens, and quiet moments of decision.

We can't fix what we won't face. As I mentioned in *Addictions and Distractions*, the first step to rebuilding anything—yourself, your family, or your community—is honesty. When men choose discipline over distraction, healing over hiding, and purpose over pain, the community begins to breathe again.

The strength of any community is measured not by its wealth, but by the wellness of its people. When we preserve ourselves, we preserve each other.

Health and Financial Consequences

The toll of addiction on physical and mental health is immense. Alcohol and drug abuse lead to chronic diseases, while excessive stress from workaholism can cause heart conditions and mental burnout. Financially, addiction can drain bank accounts, create debt, and ruin opportunities for a stable future.

Alcohol abuse, in particular, can have devastating consequences beyond personal health. Many individuals who struggle with alcoholism find themselves facing DUI (Driving Under the Influence) or DWI (Driving While Intoxicated) charges, which can lead to the loss of a driver's license, loss of employment, and even incarceration. For some, these consequences result in broken families and the inability to provide for loved ones. Substance addiction alters personality and decision-making, causing people to engage in reckless behaviors they would otherwise avoid when sober. The destruction caused by alcohol misuse is not limited to the individual, but it also affects their family, career, and community. The toll of addiction on physical and mental health is immense. Alcohol and drug abuse lead to chronic diseases, while excessive stress from workaholism can cause heart conditions and mental burnout. Financially, addiction can drain bank accounts, create debt, and ruin opportunities for a stable future.

Breaking Free

If you have an addiction, seek help. Programs like Alcoholics Anonymous (AA) for alcohol dependency or Gamblers Anonymous for gambling issues exist for a reason. Whatever your addiction may be, the first step is identifying it. If someone points it out to you, don't get defensive; chances are, they see something that you may not. Acknowledging the issue is the first step to recovery.

There is a difference between going for a walk to cool off and going to a bar and returning in the middle of the morning hours. One is a healthy way to clear your mind, while the other can lead to destructive behaviors. When dealing with stress or emotional turmoil, choosing a healthier coping mechanism can prevent addiction from taking hold and negatively impacting your life.

Whether it's setting limits on screen time, seeking professional help, or confronting personal demons, change begins with intentional action. Surrounding yourself with supportive individuals, creating healthy routines, and facing reality head-on can help break the cycle.

Freedom from addiction and distraction isn't about eliminating every pleasure; it's about regaining control. It's about making intentional choices that align with the life you want to build. The road to overcoming these struggles starts with awareness, accountability, and action. The question is: Are you ready to take that step? If you have an addiction, seek help. Programs like Alcoholics Anonymous (AA) for alcohol dependency or Gamblers Anonymous for gambling issues exist for a reason. Whatever your addiction may be, the first step is identifying it. If someone points it out to you, don't get defensive. Chances are, they see something that you may not. Acknowledging the issue is the first step to recovery.

Whether it's setting limits on screen time, seeking professional help, or confronting personal demons, change begins with intentional action. Surrounding yourself with supportive individuals, creating healthy routines, and facing reality head-on can help break the cycle.

Freedom from addiction and distraction isn't about eliminating every pleasure; it's about regaining control. It's about making intentional choices that align with the life you want to build. The road to overcoming these struggles starts with awareness, accountability, and action. The question is: Are you ready to take that step? Acknowledging the issue is the first step to recovery. Whether it's setting limits on screen time, seeking professional help, or confronting personal demons, change begins with intentional action. Surrounding yourself with supportive individuals, creating healthy routines, and facing reality head-on can help break the cycle.

Freedom from addiction and distraction isn't about eliminating every pleasure; it's about regaining control. It's about making intentional choices that align with the life you want to build. The road to overcoming these struggles starts with awareness, accountability, and action. The question is: Are you ready to take that step?

DUI-DAD – UNDER THE INFLUENCE

There are many ways a father can lose his grip on the role he is supposed to play, but one of the most common and destructive is substance abuse. Alcohol, drugs, and even the misuse of prescription medication have stolen countless men away from their children. A man may still be in the house, but his presence is not the same as his participation. Sitting in the living room with a beer in hand does not equal leadership. Driving with a child in the back seat while under the influence is not fatherhood — it is recklessness disguised as normalcy.

Children know when their father is under the influence. Even at an early age, they sense the difference in tone, mood, and energy. One day Dad may be laughing, playing games, or offering encouragement. The next day he may be slurring his words, stumbling, angry, or completely withdrawn. That kind of inconsistency teaches instability. A father becomes a stranger inside his own home — physically there but emotionally gone.

When this happens, the child begins to walk on eggshells, unsure which version of Dad will appear. In some homes, children even take on the role of the parent, trying to hide bottles, cover up embarrassing moments, or soothe tensions to keep the peace. That reversal robs children of their innocence and leaves scars that often follow them into adulthood.

Fathers caught in substance abuse often try to explain their actions away. They might say:

- "I only drink on weekends."
- "I can quit anytime I want."
- "I work hard; I deserve this."

But every excuse chips away at their credibility. A man's responsibility to his children is greater than his desire for relief. A DUI charge is not just a traffic violation — it is a flashing warning sign that the man is choosing his habits over his family. Losing a license, facing court dates, or even going to jail strips children of the stability they need. And when that happens, respect — which is hard to earn and easy to lose — begins to fade.

Every father is under some influence. The question is whether it's the influence of love, discipline, and clarity — or the influence of alcohol, drugs, and poor decisions. A father who chooses substances over sobriety teaches his children that escape is better than endurance, that numbing pain is better than solving problems, and that selfishness is acceptable.

Fathers must ask themselves: What am I showing my children about how to handle life? Because children are not only listening, they are also imitating. And when they see Dad stumble through life intoxicated, many grow up to repeat the same cycle.

For many men, substance abuse is not new; it is inherited. They grew up watching their own fathers drink too much, use drugs, or destroy relationships under the influence. Cycles like this feel normal until someone decides to break them. Choosing sobriety is not just about saving yourself; it is about creating a new story for your children. It shows them that discipline is possible, that humility in seeking help is a sign of strength, and that legacies can be rewritten.

Not every father realizes the damage while his children are still young. For some, the wake-up call comes years later, after birthdays were missed, milestones passed by, and the bond weakened under the weight of addiction. By then, those children may be adults — carrying their own scars, raising families of their own, and trying to understand why their father chose the substance over them.

Re-entering their lives is not easy. Adult children do not always welcome Dad back with open arms. Many carry resentment, distrust, or indifference. They may smile politely, but inside they are asking, "Where were you when I needed you? Why did you put the bottle, the pills, or the high before me?" That silence between father and child can feel heavier than any argument.

For the father attempting to reconnect, humility is the only doorway. Apologies must be real, consistent, and backed by change, not words. Adult children have already learned to survive without you, so what you offer now must not be empty promises but a steady presence. You cannot rewrite their childhood, but you can influence their adulthood — if you are willing to do the work, to listen more than you speak, and to respect the space they may need to heal.

It will take time. Sometimes years. And sometimes the relationship may never be fully restored. Yet even in that, the choice to stay sober, to keep showing up, and to live differently is still worth it. Because even if you cannot change the past, you can still demonstrate that cycles can end, and legacies can be redeemed.

When the Child is Now Grown

Fatherhood requires clarity. Clear thinking, clear choices, and clear priorities. A sober father is a present father. Presence does not mean perfection; it means being consistent, reliable, and available. Children may not remember the toys you bought or the money you spent, but they will never forget whether you were steady, sober, and safe when they needed you most.

The truth is simple: under the influence, you risk everything. Under clarity, you build everything. One leads to broken families, damaged respect, and generational pain. The other leads to trust, stability, and a legacy worth leaving.

It is only by the grace of God that many of us — me included — have escaped situations involving substance abuse that could have destroyed our families and scarred our children forever. Some of us have walked dangerously close to losing it all, yet by mercy we were spared. That reminder keeps us humble, grateful, and determined to never forget how fragile life can be under the weight of addiction.

A DUI dad may not realize it, but his children are watching every decision. The greatest influence a man can have is not in how much he provides while intoxicated, but in how much he protects, guides, and loves while sober.

Affirmation

I choose clarity over chaos. I choose presence over absence. I choose to break cycles, not repeat them. My children will know me as steady, sober, and safe. By God's grace, I will lead with love, discipline, and respect — never under the influence of anything but purpose.

Resources for Help

- Alcoholics Anonymous (AA): (212) 870-3400 — www.aa.org
- SAMHSA National Helpline: 1-800-662-HELP (4357) 24/7, free, confidential treatment referral and information.
- National Drug Helpline: 1-844-289-0879 — 24/7 support for drug and alcohol issues.
- National Suicide Prevention Lifeline: Dial 988 — for immediate crisis intervention and emotional support.
- National Domestic Violence Hotline: 1-800-799-SAFE (7233) for anyone experiencing domestic violence or abuse.

DWI
(DAD WHILE INCARCERATED)

Title by *Darryll Harmon*

Chapter written by and from the experience of Author
Kenneth Wigfall

Voices Through the Wire

The hardest sound in the world is silence, the kind that fills a prison cell after the phones go dead for the night.

For me, that silence always had an echo. It carried the faint sound of my children's laughter, the click of the receiver as the call ended, and the heavy reminder that I couldn't be there. Every day, every week, that silence tested me. And yet, it was that same silence that pushed me to reach out again, to call, to write, to keep that line of love alive through the walls.

Being a father behind bars isn't about distance, it's about persistence. The persistence to remain present in the lives of the people who still call you "Dad," even when they can't touch your hand or see your face except through glass. I learned quickly that relationships don't end when the gate slams shut; they just demand more work, more patience, and more heart.

The First Call

I still remember the first call home after my sentence began.

The phones were lined up along the wall, men pacing behind them like anxious ghosts waiting for their turn. Fifteen minutes, that's all we got. Fifteen minutes to fit a lifetime of questions, apologies, and love.

When I finally heard my daughter's voice, broke something open inside me.

"Daddy?" she said, cautious, like she wasn't sure if it was really me.

"Yeah, baby. It's me." My throat burned as I spoke. "How you are doing?"

There was a pause, then a small sniffle. "Mom said you can't come home for a while."

I looked around at the gray walls, the COs walking their rounds, and tried to find the right words. "That's true. I made some mistakes, and I have to fix them. But I'm still your daddy, and I love you, okay?"

She didn't answer right away. I could hear her breathing. Then, softly: "I miss you."

I swallowed hard. "I miss you too, every day. You been doing your schoolwork?"

We had a spelling test. I got nine outta ten."

"That's my girl! You are studying like I told you, huh?"

A small laugh—pure, honest, the kind that cut right through the noise of the dayroom.

That was the sound I lived for.

But right as we started to settle into the rhythm of conversation, the recorded voice cut through:

"You have one minute remaining."

That robotic reminder hit me harder than I expected.

One minute. Sixty seconds to be a father again.

"I got to go soon, baby," I said quickly. "But listen—every day, remember that Daddy loves you. Keep being good for your mom, alright? I'm proud of you."

"Okay. I love you too, Daddy."

The line clicked, and the world went silent again.

Letters: The Paper Lifeline

After that first call, I started writing letters. At first, they were awkward, too formal, too long, trying to make up for everything I couldn't say on the phone. But after a few weeks, I found a rhythm.

Letters became my visits. I poured myself into the paper—advice, memories, prayers, drawings, even jokes.

I told them about the classes I was taking inside—anger management, small business, even a GED tutoring program I volunteered in. I wanted them to see me trying to know I wasn't giving up. I told them stories about the old neighborhood, about how I used to race my bike down the hill by the park and scrape my knees, and how I'd get back up every time.

Those were the lessons I tried to give them—get back up, no matter what. Sometimes they'd write back.

My son's handwriting was messy, big letters running off the page.

He'd say things like:

"Dad, I'm playing football this year. Coach said I got a good arm."

"Mom said you're doing better. Are you coming home soon?"

"I miss you when I go to bed. I look at your picture."

Those words—simple, pure—carried more power than anything in this place.

I'd read his letters over and over until the paper got soft and the ink started to fade.

I'd fold them carefully and put them in a small box with my Bible. That was my safe place.

The Time Clock on Love

The phone system in prison doesn't care about emotions. It runs on schedules, money, and minutes.

Each call is prepaid—each second a countdown.

Fifteen minutes at a time, a father tries to stay connected to a world that keeps moving without him.

Sometimes I'd wait an hour for my turn at the phone, only to find out the number didn't go through or someone didn't pick up. Each failed call was like a small heartbreak. But on the days I got through, everything else faded away.

One afternoon, I called during my son's lunch break at school. I timed it perfectly.

"Hey, champ," I said. "How's school today?"

"Good," he said, sounding distracted. I could hear other kids in the background.

"You eating your lunch?"

"Yeah. Peanut butter again." He groaned. "Mom says it's good for me."

I laughed. "She's right. You need that energy for football."

"Dad, do you think I could make it pro one day?"

There was so much hope in that question that I had to pause.

"Anything's possible if you work for it," I said. "But remember, the most important thing is finishing school first. Sports are good, but your mind is what makes you strong."

He was quiet for a second, then said, "You talk like a teacher now."

That made me smile. Maybe I was learning something, too.

But again, the voice interrupted: "You have one minute remaining."

"Alright, champ. I got to go. But I'm proud of you, always. Keep pushing and remember—every action has a reaction. You treat people right; life will treat you right back."

"Okay, Dad. Love you."

"Love you too."

The call ended. I hung up slowly, staring at the scratched wall in front of me, thinking about how many fathers were out there doing the same thing—trying to fit a lifetime into fifteen minutes.

Outside Voices

There were days when keeping that connection felt impossible.

Some men around me had given up completely.

"They don't care about you out there," one guy said once, shaking his head as he watched me write another letter.

"They are living their lives, man. You wasting stamps."

But he didn't understand. I wasn't writing for me—I was writing for them.

Every word was a bridge.

Every letter, a reminder that I still existed in their world.

Outside influences tried to creep in too. People would tell my kids things—half-truths, gossip, or bitterness. I knew that some folks wanted them to forget about me, to believe I wasn't coming back or that I didn't care. That was the hardest part—fighting the lies with love and patience.

So, I told them the truth in every call, every letter:

"Don't let anyone tell you who your father is. If you want to know, listen to my words and watch my actions. I'm doing everything I can to be a better man for you."

That truth became my anchor.

The Rhythm of Routine

Over time, our communication found its rhythm.

I'd wake up early, grab coffee from the canteen, and sit by the window where the morning light hit just right. That's where I wrote most of my letters.

I'd start with small things—how my day went, what book I was reading, what lesson I learned in class. Then I'd ask questions:

"How's school? What subjects do you like most?"

"Who are your friends?"

"You still drawing? Still dancing?"

"What's the latest song you like?"

I learned that asking questions wasn't just about getting answers, it was about keeping their minds open, showing them, I cared about their world, not just mine.

Sometimes they'd answer in funny ways.

"Dad, we learned fractions. I don't like fractions."

"Dad, my teacher says I talk too much."

"Dad, can I send you my art project?"

I'd smile at every word, my heart swelling with pride.

I'd tell them how proud I was, how smart they were, how much potential I saw in them.

Even when the world outside was rough, I wanted my words to be a safe place.

Never Judging, Always Guiding

As they got older, the questions changed.

One day, my daughter asked over the phone, "Daddy, why did they take you away?"

That question stopped me cold. I had rehearsed this conversation a thousand times in my head, but nothing prepared me to hear it in her voice.

"I made some bad choices," I said carefully. "I broke laws I shouldn't have. And the law says when you do wrong, you have to take responsibility."

"Are you still bad?" she asked softly.

"No, baby. I'm not bad. I just did bad things. And I'm learning every day how to be better. That's why I want you to always think before you act. Every action has a reaction. That means if you make a good choice, good things happen. But if you do something wrong, you have to face the result."

There was silence, then she whispered, "Okay. I just don't want you to be sad."

"I'm not sad when I hear from you," I said. "You're my light in here."

That call stayed with me for months. It reminded me that honesty builds trust, even when the truth hurts.

Moments of Joy

Not every call was heavy.

Some days we laughed until the time ran out.

My son told me about his first crush. My daughter talked about joining the choir.

I teased them about their favorite shows, and they made fun of my old music taste.

"You still listen to them old school songs, huh, Dad?"

"Hey, that's real music! Not that noise y'all play now."

"Whatever, Dad. You're just old."

Those laughs kept me alive.

And sometimes, I'd end my letters with small pieces of wisdom—simple, steady truths:

"Be kind, even when people aren't."

"Never let anger control your choices."

"Tell the truth, even when it's hard."

"And remember—Daddy loves you, no matter where I am."

Holding the Line Against the Negative

There were temptations everywhere—to shut down emotionally, to give up when letters went unanswered, to believe the worst when the world outside went quiet.

But love is discipline. It's not about what you get back, it's about what you give, consistently, without quitting.

There were weeks when I didn't get a call. Holidays came and went.

I'd sit in my bunk, staring at the ceiling, thinking about them opening gifts without me, or sitting at the dinner table where my chair used to be. The loneliness was sharp, but it kept me humble.

On those nights, I'd write instead of sleeping.

I'd write letters I might never send, prayers for their protection, thoughts I needed to get out.

And I realized something powerful: being a father wasn't about being perfect, it was about being present in spirit.

Even from behind the wire, I could still lead, still teach, still love.

A Father's Reflection

Years passed. The calls grew deeper, the letters longer. My children began to understand more—not just about my mistakes, but about resilience, forgiveness, and faith.

They told me about their dreams. One wanted to study law; the other, music.

I told them to chase both with equal fire.

"Life's about balance," I said in one letter. "It's about knowing when to fight and when to forgive, when to speak and when to listen. Don't let the world harden your heart. And always—always—remember who you are."

Sometimes they'd write back with advice of their own.

"Dad, we're proud of you for not giving up."

"Dad, Mom said you've changed."

"When you come home, can we go fishing again?"

Reading those words was like catching a glimpse of sunrise through the bars.

What I Learned

When you're incarcerated, time moves differently. You start to measure life not by days, but by letters received, calls answered, and voices remembered. Each connection becomes sacred.

I learned that communication isn't just talking—it's listening without judgment.

It's letting your child express anger, confusion, and even disappointment without reacting defensively.

It's sharing your feelings openly, not as a man behind bars, but as a father still learning to love better.

And I learned that my children didn't need a perfect dad. They needed a consistent one.

Someone who showed up every time the phone line opened, who wrote back even when they didn't, who kept saying "I love you" even when the silence stretched too long.

Closing Reflection

As I sit here now, I can still hear their voices in my memory—sometimes laughing, sometimes crying, always reaching. Those calls, those letters, those moments of connection became the heartbeat of my rehabilitation.

They reminded me who I was, and who I still had to be.

Being a father in prison taught me that love isn't measured by distance or circumstance.

It's measured by persistence—the choice to keep showing up, keep speaking truth, keep loving no matter how thin the wire becomes.

And if there's one message, I want my children—and every child of an incarcerated parent—to hold onto, it's this:

Your parents' mistakes don't define your future.

But how we face those mistakes together, that's where healing begins.

Because every action has a reaction.

And love, no matter where it's spoken from, is still the strongest reaction of all.

The hardest sound in the world is silence, the kind that fills a prison cell after the phones go dead for the night.

For me, that silence always had an echo. It carried the faint sound of my children's laughter, the click of the receiver as the call ended, and the heavy reminder that I couldn't be there. Every day, every week, that silence tested me. And yet, it was that same silence that pushed me to reach out again, to call, to write, to keep that line of love alive through the walls.

Being a father behind bars isn't about distance, it's about persistence. The persistence to remain present in the lives of the people who still call you "Dad," even when they can't touch your hand or see your face except through glass. I learned quickly that relationships don't end when the gate slams shut; they just demand more work, more patience, and more heart.

Other work by Author *Kenneth Wigfall*

- **Nurses: Our Earthly Angels**
- **Bryson's Journey: The Key to Greatness**
- **His Gifts: How GOD has Blessed His People**
- **Shadow Visions**
- **When I Wasn't Looking: How Trouble Found Me**
- **Anew Vision**
- **Never to Late: Come On In**

Available on Amazon

SELF PRESERVATION

Self-preservation is more than survival; it is the ongoing process of safeguarding your physical, mental, emotional, and financial well-being. As men, we are often conditioned to prioritize providing for others, handling responsibilities, and pushing through hardship without complaint. However, if we fail to take care of ourselves, we limit our ability to be strong for those who depend on us. Self-preservation is about making intentional choices that support long-term stability, health, and peace of mind.

Too often, men neglect key aspects of their lives until a crisis forces them to pay attention. Whether it's ignoring health issues, failing to establish financial security, or staying in toxic relationships, neglecting self-preservation can lead to long-term consequences. This chapter explores the many facets of self-preservation—physical, financial, emotional, and spiritual—and how prioritizing these areas leads to a stronger, more fulfilled life.

The Importance of Self-Preservation

Every decision we make should be evaluated with one question in mind: Does this contribute to the preservation of my well-being? From the food we eat to the company we keep, our daily choices either sustain us or slowly deteriorate us. Prioritizing self-preservation means taking control of your future by implementing habits that promote longevity, security, and peace.

- **Physical Health:** Maintaining a strong body through exercise, proper nutrition, and regular medical checkups is crucial. Many men avoid the doctor until something is seriously wrong, but preventive care, including blood work and proper fasting before tests, can detect issues early and prevent complications.

- **Financial Stability:** Saving money, investing wisely, and avoiding unnecessary debt ensures that you're not reliant on outside sources for survival. Relying on government assistance or living paycheck to paycheck limits your ability to create a secure future for yourself and your family.

- **Emotional and Mental Well-being:** Stress, anxiety, and unresolved trauma can weigh a man down if left unchecked. Setting boundaries, evaluating relationships, and creating work-life balance help prevent burnout and maintain a strong mental state.

- **Spiritual Growth:** No matter what your beliefs are, having a keen sense of purpose and connection to something greater than yourself can bring clarity and stability. Whether through faith, meditation, or mindfulness, spiritual self-preservation is key to inner peace.

By taking control of these aspects of life, men can ensure they are not just surviving but thriving. This chapter will dive deeper into each area, providing practical ways to protect and improve the foundation of your well-being.

Physical Health and Nutrition

Your body is the first line of defense in self-preservation. Strength starts long before you ever lift a weight—it begins with how you treat yourself every day. Too many men wait until pain, fatigue, or illness forces them to take action. Preventive care is not weakness—it's wisdom. The man who makes time for his health today won't be forced to make time for illness tomorrow.

Make it a habit to **know your numbers**—blood pressure, cholesterol, glucose, weight, and waist size. These are your warning lights, the same way a dashboard tells you when your car needs attention. Men usually work and juggle a lot, so health often gets pushed to the side. But remember this: the same body that provides, protects, and performs needs proper maintenance too. Going to the doctor more than once a year and getting full blood work can be life-saving. **Early detection is critical—especially as you age.**

Most medical providers now offer **patient portals** like *MyChart* that allow you to see test results and notes in one place. Use them to track your numbers and hold yourself accountable.

Now, let's be honest—I get it. I have allergies, so I'm not exactly a foodie. And there's nothing like a good burger and fries, or some oxtails with rice and peas, or tacos that fall apart when you bite them. I understand that completely. But at some point, you have to cut back on all that—not eliminate it, just balance it.

Exercise is natural for us as men. We ran around as kids—through sports, games, or just burning off energy. But as we get older, we get busier, and all we want to do is sit around instead of run around.

That can be dangerous. Walking 30 minutes a day, doing push-ups, stretching—these small habits add up. As I mentioned in *Addictions and Distractions*, your daily habits will either heal you or hurt you.

Don't be too hard on yourself. I'm no physical specimen by any stretch of the imagination. The main thing is awareness and progress—working toward these things a little at a time. As you get older, your limits change, and that's okay. Your health is mostly tied to your behavior, and behavior is one of the hardest things to change. The goal is to keep showing up and making adjustments as you go. Consistency beats perfection every time.

Financial Self-Preservation

Money can be both a tool and a trap. It's one of the greatest tests of discipline a man will ever face. Saving even a small amount regularly builds the muscle of preparation. Emergencies, opportunities, and transitions all come easier when you're financially ready.

Avoid living beyond your means or trying to impress others. Pride and comparison have destroyed more budgets than poverty ever will. The car, the watch, or the clothes don't define you—discipline does. **Debt robs your future and steals your peace.** Learn to budget, invest, and think long-term.

Oftentimes, as men, we spend out of appearance. There's so much pressure on us to look like we have it all together—to appear strong, successful, and in control—even when we're struggling behind the scenes. But that appearance can become the very thing that breaks you. Don't find yourself fifteen or twenty years from now saying, *"Damn, I blew my money on bullshit."* Regret is expensive, and time doesn't give refunds.

Financial self-preservation also means protecting yourself from the unexpected. Have proper insurance, maintain good credit, and understand your numbers. Money should work for you—not the other way around.

Remember what we discussed in *Genetic Reset*—breaking generational habits starts with personal discipline. The man who manages $100 wisely will handle $10,000 the same way. Financial freedom doesn't begin in your wallet—it begins in your mindset.

Friendships and Relationships

The people you surround yourself with will either drain your energy or help you grow. Not everyone deserves access to your peace. Evaluate your friendships honestly. Are they adding value, or pulling you into negativity, gossip, and chaos?

As men, we often confuse **loyalty with longevity**—keeping people around just because we've known them for years. Real loyalty is rooted in respect and accountability. A friend who values you will challenge you, not enable you.

I encourage you to look within and be honest with yourself. Sometimes the issue isn't them—it's you. Having boundaries with friends doesn't make you exempt from accountability. A healthy man doesn't just expect respect—he gives it. He listens, apologizes when necessary, and corrects himself when he's wrong, even if the other party insists otherwise. Always be responsible for the man in the mirror and be true to him.

As we learned in *Victory, Not Violence*, emotional control and awareness are key. The same discipline that keeps you from reacting in anger will keep you from sabotaging your relationships.

Sometimes, protecting your peace means stepping back from certain environments. That's not arrogance, it's self-preservation.

Doctor Visits and Preventive Care

Men have a habit of toughing it out. We'll ignore pain, skip appointments, and say, "I'm fine," even when we're not. But prevention is easier than repair. The strongest thing a man can do is catch a problem before it becomes one.

Schedule annual physicals and get your full blood work done. Fast properly before tests so your results are accurate. Don't ignore warning signs—headaches, fatigue, shortness of breath, changes in weight, appetite, or mood. Those are your body's alarms. Listening early can save your life later.

As we age, **certain screenings become non-negotiable**. Two of the most important—and most avoided—are **colonoscopy** and **prostate checks**. Both are vital for men, especially after 40. Colon cancer and prostate cancer are silent killers that often show no symptoms until it's too late.

A **colonoscopy** is recommended starting around age 45, sometimes earlier if there's family history. It's not pleasant to think about, but it's far less painful than the consequences of ignoring it. One short procedure can detect and even remove pre-cancerous polyps before they turn into something serious.

Prostate exams are another major step in protecting your health. Your doctor may check your prostate manually or through a PSA (Prostate-Specific Antigen) blood test. Many men avoid this conversation out of embarrassment, but embarrassment doesn't save lives—action does. If something doesn't feel right when you urinate, or you notice pain, swelling, or unusual symptoms, talk to your doctor immediately.

Use tools like **MyChart** or other health apps to track these results and monitor your progress. Don't wait for someone else to remind you. Set your own reminders. Take control of your health story.

Build a relationship with your doctor, not just a quick visit when you're sick. Ask questions, take notes, and understand what's being said. If you don't feel respected or heard, find another provider. You are the advocate for your own body.

As mentioned earlier in *Physical Health and Nutrition*, your health is your responsibility. A strong man isn't just the one who lifts the most weight—he's the one who has the courage to take care of himself. There's nothing weak about being proactive. It's one of the most mature decisions you can make because it means you plan to be here for the long run—for your family, your purpose, and your peace.

Spiritual and Emotional Balance

Self-preservation isn't just about what you can see, it's also about what you feel and believe. Spiritual balance doesn't require religion; it requires reflection. Take time to slow down, to listen, and to be still. Whether it's through prayer, meditation, nature, or gratitude, connecting to something greater keeps your spirit aligned when life gets heavy.

As mentioned earlier in *Victory, Not Violence*, awareness is power. That same awareness applies here—being in tune with what's happening inside of you. Many men focus so much on surviving that they never stop to ask themselves if they're truly living. You can have money, strength, and position, yet still feel empty inside if your spirit is unbalanced. Peace doesn't come from possessions—it comes from perspective.

A spiritual foundation keeps you from drifting. It gives meaning to both your struggles and your victories. Whether you call it faith, energy, or purpose, it's what reminds you that your life is part of something larger. It grounds you when life tests your patience, and it humbles you when pride tries to take over. Some of the best conversations you'll ever have won't be with another person—they'll be between you and God, or you and your conscience. That's where honesty lives.

Emotional balance is just as important. It means setting boundaries and recognizing that you are not responsible for managing everyone else's emotions. Don't let other people's chaos become your storm. Learn to say no without guilt and yes without fear. Protect your peace, because when your mind and spirit are clear, your decisions become sharper.

As we discussed in *Addictions and Distractions*, it's easy to drown out emotions with work, entertainment, or substances. But avoidance isn't healing. True strength is facing your feelings head-on—anger, fear, disappointment—and learning to respond, not react. Emotional discipline is a form of self-respect.

In today's world, we talk a lot about **A.I.—artificial intelligence.** But as technology keeps advancing, so must your **E.I.—emotional intelligence.** Machines may learn to think faster, but they'll never learn to feel deeper. Your ability to understand your emotions, read the room, and show empathy will separate you from those who only operate logically. Emotional intelligence is what keeps men grounded, compassionate, and aware in a world that's becoming more automated by the day. It's not just about knowing how you feel, it's about knowing how to manage it, and how your actions affect others.

Always allow yourself to feel how you feel—and, more importantly, allow others to do the same. Emotions aren't weakness; they're information. But don't make permanent decisions based on temporary feelings. Give space to those around you who make emotional decisions; they may be acting from pain you don't fully see. You may have to decide to forgive them or ask for their forgiveness. Both are signs of strength, not surrender.

There will be days when you feel disconnected or lost; that's part of being human. When that happens, slow down. Revisit the practices that restore you. Talk to a trusted friend, take a walk, pray, write, or simply sit in silence. The goal isn't perfection—it's peace.

Remember: **a man at peace is a man in control.** When your emotions and spirit are aligned, your purpose becomes clearer, your relationships grow healthier, and your outlook becomes steadier. Spiritual and emotional balance doesn't make you soft—it makes you solid.

In Closing

Self-preservation is not selfish, it's strategy. It's saying, "I can't pour from an empty cup." The man who preserves himself can provide more, give more, and lead better. The goal is not perfection—it's consistency. Small, intentional steps each day add up to a lifetime of strength, stability, and peace.

NO DESIRE TO BE RIGHT

"If loving you is wrong, I don't want to be right"—a song composed by Luther Ingram in 1972—tells the story of a married man with two children having an affair. Everyone was against him, and rightly so. While the song may not be the best example of the principle I want to convey—since it involves a clear violation of adultery—it does bring up an interesting perspective.

As men, we often have a strong desire to be right, but in my opinion, we should abandon this desire in favor of what works. Of course, this doesn't mean disregarding moral principles or breaking the law—if something violates ethical or legal boundaries, it cannot truly work in your favor. However, there are many situations where doing what works may go against the opinions or beliefs of others. Leadership, in particular, requires the ability to focus on solutions rather than personal validation. You don't always have to be the one who comes up with the winning idea.

Self-Reflection and Change

At times, introspection is necessary, looking within and honestly assessing whether your current approach is working for you. A simple way to measure this is by evaluating your progress.

For example, if you work year after year but struggle to save money or get ahead, something isn't working. It's time to reassess and adjust. If staying out all night, being late for work, and risking your job is not serving you, change your habits. If hanging with a group of aimless friends who engage in trouble isn't leading you anywhere positive, it's time to reconsider your circle.

Another thing I've noticed is how often men argue about things that don't matter. Let it go. If someone's opinion works for them, let them have it. Winning a verbal debate won't make a difference in your real life. What truly matters is what's happening inside your castle, your personal space, your household, your business, and your close relationships.

Setting Boundaries and Doing What Works

Don't be afraid to go against the grain. People will often tell you what they think is "right" for you, even though they don't live your life and don't know your circumstances. That doesn't mean you should reject advice—just make sure it comes from people who understand your reality, not those who want to sound wise. I once heard someone say, *"Never take marriage advice from someone who's never been married."* There's truth in that statement. Even failed marriages can teach valuable lessons. Sometimes mistakes provide the best wisdom because they show you what not to repeat.

As men, we often carry an ego that convinces us being wrong—or even appearing wrong—means we've lost something. We equate being corrected with being disrespected. That mindset keeps us stuck in cycles of pride and defensiveness. The truth is, **you don't lose when you're wrong—you lose when you refuse to learn.**

There's power in saying, "I didn't get that right." There's growth in admitting, "I could've handled that differently." Admitting fault doesn't make you less of a man—it makes you more of one. Real strength isn't about proving people wrong; it's about improving yourself.

It's wild how much energy grown men waste trying to be right. Some will spend hours arguing over which player or team is better, as if their voice on social media or at the bar changes the score. They'll sit in man caves or barbershops, pounding the table in the name of debate about a game they'll never play or a move they could never make. Many of us have turned arguing into a hobby and started calling it "passion."

The same thing plays out on a larger stage. Look at politics—rooms full of men standing for hours in filibusters, engaging in verbal tug-of-war, wasting time, and calling it democracy. It's the same competition happening in living rooms and bars across the country: a battle of who can talk the longest instead of who can listen the best.

The problem isn't discussion—it's obsession. The constant need to be right distracts from doing what works. What works for you may not work for someone else, and that's perfectly fine. Maturity means knowing when to stop arguing and start acting.

As a business owner, I've had to make choices that fit my life and not someone else's expectations. People often ask why I don't bid on government jobs. My answer is simple: most of them are **net 90**, meaning I do the job today and don't get paid for 90 days. That schedule doesn't fit my company. It's not about right or wrong—it's about what aligns with my system and goals.

When you understand your limits, goals, and capacity, you stop trying to force yourself into spaces that weren't designed for you. Boundaries aren't barriers—they're blueprints. They help you stay aligned with your peace, your values, and your vision.

As I mentioned in *Self-Preservation*, setting boundaries isn't selfish—it's survival. Boundaries protect your peace, your time, and your purpose. You can't please everyone, and you're not meant to. Doing what works for you isn't rebellion—it's responsibility.

And as life changes, so should your methods. What worked for you five years ago might not work today. Be conscious, not stiff-necked. Adjust when necessary. Pride says, "I'll keep doing it my way." Wisdom says, "If it's not working, it's time to pivot."

The goal isn't to always be right—it's to be real, adaptable, and at peace. That's where strength truly lives. When you can admit, adjust, and advance, you win—not the argument, but your life.

Boundaries That Evolve

Setting boundaries is crucial, and you can't be afraid to establish them from the very beginning. Many relationships—personal, professional, and even family—suffer because clear boundaries were never set. It's not about selfishness; it's about self-awareness.

I've often heard people say they did something for someone, only to be ignored when they needed a favor in return. That's why setting boundaries early is essential, it prevents disappointment later. When expectations are unclear, frustration fills the gap. Clear boundaries help protect both sides from confusion and resentment.

Boundaries teach people how to treat you, and they also teach you how to manage your time and energy. Without them, frustration builds silently until it eventually shows up as anger, withdrawal, or burnout. When you know your limits, you can give freely without feeling drained or taken for granted.

As someone who travels frequently, I no longer enjoy long drives. I once drove 24 hours from Florida to New York, and today, I wouldn't be entertained by that idea for 30 seconds. Does that make me wrong? Absolutely not. What law am I breaking by choosing a two-hour flight over a 24-hour drive? None. That choice simply reflects who I am today and what works for me now.

If you're just learning this—like I did later in life—it's okay to go back and set boundaries now. You can't change how people responded in the past; you can only teach them how to engage with you moving forward. It doesn't have to be dramatic; it just has to be clear.

Sometimes that means saying something like:

"I realize I've always said yes to things that stretched me too thin. I'm learning to manage my time and energy better, so I might not always be available the same way I used to be."

Or maybe:

"I appreciate our friendship, and I need to pull back from conversations that leave me drained. It's nothing personal—I'm protecting my peace."

Simple, honest, and direct. Boundaries don't require an argument—they only require follow-through.

As discussed in *Self-Preservation*, peace often comes from knowing what drains you and what sustains you. At the same time, as I shared in *Willing to Be Used*, there's a difference between being **useful** and being **used up**. You can serve others without sacrificing yourself.

Boundaries shift as you grow. The things that once made sense may no longer fit where you are in life—and that's okay. Too many men cling to old habits or outdated routines out of pride; afraid someone will say they've "changed." Growth requires change. If it no longer works, adjust.

Boundaries don't just protect your time; they protect your mindset. They give you permission to evolve, to prioritize what matters most, and to say "no" without guilt.

When you honor your boundaries, you create space for clarity, respect, and genuine connection. The man who knows his limits isn't weak—he's wise.

Leadership and What Works

True leaders focus on what works for them and their team, rather than what is merely perceived as right. Ingram's song suggests that he didn't care what people thought—though in his case, he was breaking a moral and legal boundary. That's not the kind of man I aspire to be. But the underlying lesson still holds: move with purpose, focus on solutions, and prioritize what truly works over the need to be right.

Collateral Damage

As a man, you will be responsible for assessing damage, whether or not you were the procuring cause. Just chalk it up as friendly fire.

After your assessment, recognize what you could have done differently, make the necessary repairs, and move on. Remember, the fight is always for 360 degrees of peace. You should be intentional about seeking peace in all aspects of your life. Everywhere you go, with everyone you engage, your goal should be to bring peace to the situation—by any means necessary.

The opposite of peace is war. In the event you need to use force, be the first at it. However, always avoid physical force. Instead, lean on mental and intellectual strength to restore peace. These are the attributes of a man, in my opinion—not to manipulate or control, but to create peace.

Understanding will often be based on the result you desire, both in the present and the future. Look ahead and execute with precision and purpose. Once you can replicate this in all four zones of your life, you will experience the peace you seek.

The Four Zones of Life

1. **Self-care**
2. **Community care**
3. **Family care**
4. **Career care**

These zones often overlap, bringing you to a full 360-degree sense of peace. Throughout this book, I will discuss the moving parts within these zones. By the time you finish reading, I encourage you to read it again—this time with a deeper understanding of the ultimate goal of peace all around you. Then, read it again with other men, helping one another develop and refine even better ideas to become stronger and more complete individuals.

The Battle Within

I must acknowledge that peace may be intermittent, especially in the early phases of life. At times, it may even seem impossible to obtain. This struggle often stems from the internal battle with your ego. The ego will have its own plan and may take a different stance depending on the situation and the zone you are operating in. If left unchecked, this leads to what I call self-destruction.

The signs of self-destruction appear early in life when someone who knows you well—perhaps even better than you know yourself—makes a suggestion based on a pattern of behavior they have noticed. In youth, it's common to dismiss such advice. However, based on my experience and reflection, I suggest suppressing the ego. Give yourself the time and space to evaluate the observation. Be honest with yourself about what you don't yet understand and make the necessary changes. Some adjustments may be immediate, while others may take time.

Know that the ego often tells you to reject the advice of those who know you best. These individuals understand that peace is more important than war.

A Lesson in Discipline

As a child, I remember a time when my high school football coach, Coach Frank Brown, questioned why I had missed practice the previous day. Although I could have informed him in advance, I chose not to, as I had a job interview that might have conflicted with my practice schedule.

The next day, as I walked through the hallway between classes, Coach Brown called out to me—what sounded like a yell at the time.

"Harmon! Why weren't you at practice yesterday?"

I replied, "I had something to do."

With the same intensity, Coach followed up: "Are you going to be there today?"

At that point, I had not yet received an offer from the interview, so I responded, "Yes."

Coach then stated in a firm tone, "You're gonna get the wood."

To those who know, they know. At that moment, I knew my high school football career had ended. The last game ball I wiped off in the rain would be the last one I ever touched. Coach meant business, and I understood the consequences of missing practice.

Breaking the Cycle

As I got older, I noticed that my grandfather always spoke loudly. Later in life, I realized he wasn't necessarily yelling—he simply had a loud way of speaking. As I grew, I carried this same habit.

One day, my children confronted me about it, and I can only imagine that my tone triggered a feeling of flight rather than engagement. What I wanted was for them to listen, but my approach had the opposite effect. It was then that I recognized the need to lower my voice. Just as I hadn't liked being yelled at, my children didn't respond well to it either.

Even now, I remain conscious of the volume at which I speak and the way others speak to me. Yelling can resurface old wounds in a person, making them shut down rather than engage. This small shift in awareness makes a significant impact on relationships and, ultimately, on maintaining peace.

By striving to master these elements in all four zones of life, you can create and sustain the peace you desire. It takes effort, discipline, and the willingness to evolve, but the reward is a life of balance and fulfillment.

WILLING TO BE USED

Are You Willing to Be Used?

Being a man is not easy. Too often, we get the short end of the stick—facing false accusations, scandals, and stereotypes that do not define who we truly are. But this is not a message of making excuses. Instead, it's a challenge—a call to rise above it all like so often we as men do.

At some point in your life, you will be asked: **Are you willing to be used?** It may not be framed in those exact words, but the calling will be there—the responsibility to do more, to be more.

Not all of us will be called to the level of **Dr. Martin Luther King Jr.**, who wanted equality for all, he gave his life so that we could have freedom. His reward? A holiday, some statues—yet he wished for a long life like any other man as he stated in his Mountain Top Speech.

Not all of us will be like **Malcolm X**, who built confidence in Black and Brown people at a time when identity was a struggle. At some point, he must have realized he had reached the point of no return. Yet he kept his hand on the plow understanding the assignment, with a wife and kids he stood tall in the face of adversity for the benefit of the lease of these.

But the question remains: **Are you willing to be used?**

Our families need us. Our communities need us. There are kids out there who need us.

Are you willing to be used **like John Brown? Like Nelson Mandela? Like Jackie Robinson?** History remembers men who stood against the odds—men like **A. Philip Randolph, Richard Loving, William Lewis Moore, Peter George Norman,** and so many others. These men didn't wait for permission. They didn't ask, *What's in it for me?* They saw a need and stepped forward.

We don't need to be these men or match their sacrifice, but we must be willing to be used for the betterment of mankind. They did what was needed at that time. This time requires something different: coming together as men, and putting our differences aside, which in most cases is the likeness of a particular team. The heavy lifting has been done. Now it is time for precision planning and execution. Go out, join an organization, and help out, just be present and be willing to be used when called on. There are a lot of organizations doing the hands-on work, and they need volunteers. You may never actually be called on; that's not the point of this message. The point is to be willing, be ready, and be present.

Are You the Best You Can Be?

- **Are you the best son you can be?**
  Maybe you've been told "no" more times than you think is fair. But that doesn't mean you stop being a son. Your mother might need you now. Your father might need you. Maybe it's not your parents; it could be a mentor, an elder, a friend. Be a son to someone who needs you.

- **Are you the best father you can be?**
  So, what if you've made mistakes? So, what if you just got out of prison after a 10- or 20-year sentence? Maybe you're still locked up. **Call your kids.** Arrange a meeting. Be present. Let them say what they need to say. Listen. Allow yourself to be used in their lives.

- **Are you the best brother you can be?**
  When was the last time you spoke to your brother or sister? What is so important that you can't put it behind you? Even if you think you're right, let **it go.** Be a peacemaker. Let yourself be used for love and kindness.

- **Are you the best coach you can be?**
  Your players may only get encouragement from you. If someone asked them about your impact, what would they say? Did you inspire them? Did you lift them up when they doubt themselves?'

- **Are you the best Uncle you can be?** Oh, let me guess, you are mad at your brother or sister, but your niece and nephews need to hear another voice of encouragement. Are you willing to speak to them? Are you willing to listen to them?

I have so many who have poured into me, and maybe you are like me in that so many have poured into you, even when you were out to be the worst version of yourself you could be. Is it possible you haven't reached that point yet, but don't know which way to go? I'm convinced that the community will always need encouragement and lifting up, so I don't only write for the current, I also include eternity, and allow myself to be used.

The Work Is Hard, and the Reward Is Small—Do It Anyway.

The work is heavy. The reward and recognition are often small. **But will that stop you?**

Are you the type of man who says, "That's not my business," or do you believe it takes a village to raise a child, to build a community? I'm not suggesting putting yourself in harm's way, volunteering to read at the school, standing tall and bold, be the man that so many don't see at home. Encourage your buddies to also do the same. Willing to be used, in a new way.

Dr. Martin Luther King Jr. once told the story of **Jericho Road** the night before he was assassinated. A man had fallen into a ditch. He was injured. He needed help. But many passed him by because the area had a bad reputation. They feared it was a setup, a trap. Yet one man stopped—one man was willing to be used.

Are you that man?

Are you the man who will help the widow and her children?

Are you the man who will step up for the single mother without expecting anything in return?

Are you the man who will put down the video game controller, get a second job, and provide for his family?

Are you the man who will sacrifice a weekend with the fellas to clean out the spare room so your wife can finally start that craft business she's been dreaming of?

I won't lie to you, the reward **on Earth** is small.

You will feel used.

You will feel unappreciated.

You will feel like it's not fair.

But I say this with humility—that's okay.

Because others before you have risked everything.

And even now, there are men out there **willingly** laying down their lives for their families and their communities, with little to no reward.

The question is: **Are you willing to be used?**

GET OFF MY LAWN

The phrase "Get Off My Lawn" has long been associated with older men shaking their fists at the younger generation, expressing frustration at how times have changed. But beyond the literal meaning, this sentiment reflects a deeper struggle between generations—the feeling of disconnection, the resistance to change, and the challenge of maintaining relevance in an evolving world. Men often find themselves at a crossroads, where experience and wisdom clash with the new ways of thinking brought in by younger generations. Instead of widening this gap, there's an opportunity to bridge it through understanding, respect, and shared learning.

The Generational Gap

Every generation believes they had it harder and did things "the right way." The older generation often looks at younger men and thinks they lack discipline, work ethic, and resilience, while younger men see the older generation as stuck in outdated ways, unwilling to adapt to modern times. This clash is natural—each generation is shaped by different experiences, economies, and cultural influences.

Technology has played a huge role in shaping the younger generation, making information more accessible but also creating a culture of instant gratification. Parenting styles have also shifted, with more emphasis on emotional intelligence and mental health, whereas older generations often valued toughness and self-reliance above all else. While both approaches have their merits, the key is to find common ground rather than dismissing each other's perspectives outright.

Respect or Resentment?

One of the biggest struggles for older men is the feeling of being overlooked or undervalued in a world that idolizes youth. Some feel they've put in their years of work, earned their stripes, and deserve respect simply because of that. But younger men may not see it that way—they respect action over entitlement.

Respect is not automatically given; it is earned through leadership, wisdom, and presence. Older men who actively invest in younger generations—by mentoring, guiding, and teaching—naturally command respect. On the other hand, those who constantly belittle or dismiss younger men's experiences create resentment rather than admiration.

Younger men must also recognize that experience holds value. Just because an older man's way of doing things may seem outdated doesn't mean it lacks wisdom. Instead of writing off their perspectives, it's beneficial to listen, adapt, and apply what works in today's world.

Lessons from the Past

History repeats itself when lessons aren't passed down effectively. Many struggles faced by younger men today—financial hardship, family dynamics, personal growth—mirror those that older men once navigated. The key is to share these lessons without forcing them onto the younger generation.

Some principles are timeless:

- Hard work and discipline still yield results.
- Family and community matter.
- Integrity and respect will always open doors.

However, the way these principles are applied changes with the times. Instead of trying to recreate the past, older men should focus on adapting these lessons to today's world, ensuring their wisdom is both relevant and impactful.

Building Bridges Instead of Fences

Instead of widening the generational divide, men can work to bridge it. Open conversations, mutual respect, and mentorship play key roles in creating a balanced relationship between old and young. Instead of dismissing younger men as lazy or weak, take the time to understand their challenges. Instead of assuming older men are out of touch, younger men should seek their guidance and apply their wisdom in modern ways.

Mentorship is one of the most powerful tools available to strengthen families, communities, and friendships. An older man who takes the time to mentor a younger one creates a ripple effect—those lessons get passed down for generations. It's about leading by example, showing resilience, and being present rather than just offering criticism.

Listening is just as important as speaking. Both generations have something to teach one another, but if no one is willing to listen, nothing gets learned.

Stuck on Stage

There's a moment in every man's life where he has to ask himself—Am I living in the present, or am I stuck in the past? Many of us get caught performing the same act, stuck in roles we played decades ago, talking about the "good old days" as if that's the only version of life we knew how to live. That's what it means to be stuck on stage.

You see it everywhere—from the barbershop to sports debates, to political conversations, and even in the workplace. Instead of acknowledging the brilliance of today's talents, we cling to comparisons from the past. Athletes today are immediately stacked up against legends from the '80s and '90s. Performers are rarely allowed to stand on their own because we're too busy trying to measure them by standards set generations ago. Even politicians are framed through the lens of those who came before them. And while reflection has its place, living in the past prevents us from appreciating the present.

Men especially fall into this trap. We replay our greatest hits—the days when we were stronger, faster, more admired, more needed. Like performers who can't let go of their prime, we keep returning to the same old act, even when the stage has changed. The spotlight fades, but we're still there, trying to move the way we once did, expecting the same applause, even when our audience and our relevance have shifted.

The danger in staying stuck on stage is that you miss the beauty of the current moment. You miss the chance to create something new, something real. Life is not a rerun. You are not the same man you were back then, and that's not a terrible thing. Growth isn't supposed to keep you performing; it's supposed to free you.

There's power in stepping off that stage and being honest about where you are now. You may not move like you used to, but that doesn't mean you can't move forward. Maybe you don't have the same spotlight, but now you have wisdom. Maybe your stage is smaller—but it's more authentic.

This doesn't mean you forget your past. It means you stop being trapped by it. Honor your history without letting it hold you hostage. Your story isn't over, and your relevance didn't expire with your youth. Learn how to perform with the grace of your present strength, not the illusion of your past glory.

And remember—real growth isn't about pretending you're still who you used to be. It's about learning to be fully present in who you are right now.

That includes how we handle confrontation. In our younger days, we may have responded to disrespect or disagreement with aggression, ego, or the need to prove ourselves. Now, maturity teaches us that every battle isn't worth fighting. Real strength is knowing when to speak, when to listen, and when to walk away. That's not weakness, that's wisdom.

The same goes for how we once moved through relationships. Maybe back in the day, we prided ourselves on how many women we could pursue, how many phone numbers we had saved, or how easily we could charm our way into someone's life. But now? Real manhood recognizes the value in building, not chasing. One meaningful connection is worth more than a dozen shallow ones. Running around gets old—and so do we.

At some point, you stop needing to prove that you *still got it* and start asking yourself if what you have is actually worth keeping. And when you find peace in that question, you'll realize—stepping off that old stage doesn't mean you're done performing. It just means you're finally choosing a role that fits who you truly are.

Conclusion

The phrase "Get Off My Lawn" can represent resistance to change or frustration with younger generations. But rather than holding onto that mentality, men must learn to adapt, lead, and share wisdom. Clinging to resentment only isolates you from those who could benefit from your experience.

The challenge for men of all ages is clear: build up, don't tear down. Respect is a two-way street, and understanding goes a long way in keeping generations connected. The real legacy of a man isn't in how well he protected his lawn—it's in how well he guided those who walked on it.

THAT BAG

Generational Wealth

S**shhh**: So a man speaks as he thinks. What is your plan to build generational wealth, or better yet, inheritance? What will you inherit upon the death of your loved ones, usually your parents? This is part of the issue—too much talk and no action. Doing basic things with basic results but expecting extraordinary longevity.

Let's look at the origin of generational wealth. It's a biblical principle. The first thing to notice is that the word itself is **plural**, meaning it should be **multiplied**. Now, what are we multiplying? How much will one generation need before they run out? Or better yet, how much will they need to sustain the next two generations? Keep in mind—the generation after them should already be provided for.

The reality is, no matter what your background, there is a **65% chance or greater** that you were not left with generational wealth. Regardless of race, inheritance is not a common reality for many. Let's put it into perspective, one generation at $1 million is just a starting point. If you weren't left anything, start where you can.

Investments to Consider

Life Insurance

Make sure you have a **term life insurance policy** for your kids. A rule of thumb is to match your mortgage balance with your coverage so that your primary residence is paid off if something happens to you. For example, if your mortgage balance is $300,000, your life insurance should be at least $300,000. Consult with a **qualified** life insurance agent—**TikTok is not a financial planner.**

IUL (Indexed Universal Life Insurance) is gaining traction because of its borrowing power. However, depending on your age, this may or may not be for you. I strongly recommend this for the youth.

Consult a licensed financial planner. There are other financial vehicles that can move the needle closer to generational wealth. But understand this—mattress money and savings accounts alone do **not** equal generational wealth.

Real Estate: The Leading Investment

In the best-case scenario, you will be left **property**. In the worst-case scenario, you will sell the property you were left. But for most people, **you weren't left anything to sell or keep.**

Back in the day, people did **more with less** because they stuck together and had **buying power**. I can't emphasize enough the **power of two**, whether it be spouses, business partners, or siblings investing together.

If you inherit a property but it wasn't **deeded properly**, seek a **financial planner**. If you are 65 or older, **you should not be holding assets in your name**; they should already be deeded to your beneficiaries. You can easily do this and **remain in the property with a life estate**, meaning no one can remove you or sell the property while you are alive. Consult a **life estate attorney**.

The Long Game

When we talk about getting to the bag, it's easy to focus only on what we can see — the job, the hustle, or the next contract. We chase the check, but too often we forget about what happens *after* we get it. Having money is one thing; managing it wisely is another.

There are many ways to build and protect your financial foundation: saving consistently, budgeting, investing in yourself, and finding income streams that make sense for your lifestyle. The one area I haven't talked much about is **stocks**. There was a time when investing in the stock market meant calling a broker and needing thousands of dollars just to get started. That time has passed.

Today, with just a smartphone and a little discipline, you can invest directly through apps and online platforms. You can purchase full shares or even **fractions** of shares in major companies — meaning you can start small and still build over time. There are now more vehicles to grow your money than ever before.

I encourage you to **study this for yourself.** Read, research, and learn the basics before you jump in. Add stocks to your portfolio, and if you don't have one yet, start one. It's not about getting rich overnight; it's about consistency and education. The goal is to make your money work while you rest.

The same way you wouldn't skip a workout for your physical health, don't skip financial training for your future. Learn to balance earning, saving, investing, and spending with purpose. Every man should have something that grows while he sleeps — because stability isn't built on effort alone; it's built on strategy.

Wills and Trusts: Protect Your Assets

Make sure you have a **will and a trust** in place. This includes:

- **Medical power of attorney**
- **Estate planning**
- **Asset protection**

This is **bonus material**, but crucial to sustaining wealth. Once you have secured a primary residence—or even if you haven't yet—**get income-producing property.**

How do you do that? Study real estate. There's too much to include here but just know this—**real estate is the leading investment.**

Purchase the book "Trust the Process" By Attorney Shannon Wright. This book can be found on Amazon.

One downside is that **real estate is not liquid,** meaning you can't sell it instantly like stocks. **Stocks are liquid assets**; they can be sold for cash quickly, minus fees. **Understand the difference.**

Residual Income and Passive Wealth

Any **residual business** where the **numbers look right** should be considered. If you have to work to get paid, that's just making money; it's **not** generational wealth. **Start where you can**, but at the very least, **ensure your life** so that your family is covered.

Important: Get a **medical exam** when purchasing life insurance so that your policy **goes into effect immediately.** Without a medical exam, **you won't be covered for the first two years.** If you die within those two years, your family won't receive the full policy amount.

Debt, Expenses, and Financial Discipline

Keep your expenses to a minimum. As you get older, start eliminating debt. Let **passive income** pay for your future investments. Keep working, don't relax. Get up every morning and **do what got you where you are.** As a man, you will **always** create new challenges for yourself—unless you were just talking.

We are **all selfish**—I believe that, and not much would change my mind about it. But **there is a difference between being selfish and being self-centered.** Being selfish is sometimes necessary for survival. **Being self-centered** means you refuse to sacrifice for others. If you die without leaving your kids **anything**, you are **self-centered. I can't tell you how often I hear, I'm not leaving those ungrateful kids or family members anything.

At a minimum, leave your family:

1. **A paid-off house**
2. **A bank account with at least $50K after burial expenses**
3. **No outstanding bills**

"I Just Ain't Got It Right Now"

If you don't have enough money to start building wealth, **make sure you aren't spending money on unnecessary things:**

- **Lottery tickets (including scratch-offs)**
- **Cigarettes**

- **Weed**
- **Gym membership you don't use**
- **Streaming subscriptions you don't need**
- **Multiple cars**
- **Multiple girlfriends**
- **Spending money on a dream while your kids are uncovered**
- **Eating out excessively**
- **Cigars**
- **Multiple vacations a year**
- **Alcohol**
- **Betting**
- **Video Games**
- **Buy less Christmas gifts**
- **Have a smaller wedding**

The Impact of the Vietnam War on Generational Wealth

The **Vietnam War (1955-1975)** reshaped family structures in America. Before the war, families stuck together, life was simple yet structured, and wealth-building was **intentional**. But as war casualties, substance abuse, and economic hardships increased, **families started breaking apart**. The **priorities shifted.**

By the **1960s and 1970s**, many people experienced **shame, depression, and addiction.** Drug and alcohol use **skyrocketed**, and family wealth took a major hit.

Fast forward to **1981**—when **crack cocaine hit the streets**. This became a major **reset button** on generational wealth, particularly for low-income communities, disrupting financial stability for generations to come.

Many families spent money on the children of substance users instead of saving for future generations. While they may have benefited from the wisdom of their grandparents, the financial struggle remained evident.

Those who were supposed to inherit wealth, the children of the **1970s and 1980s**—were often **not mentally stable enough to manage it**. Many were either **addicted to drugs or surrounded by those who were.**

Many will challenge me on this and say there were other factors at play—not everyone was on drugs or directly affected by them, and I would agree. However, the core issue remains: the family structure has been disrupted, and it is much harder for a struggling individual to leave an inheritance compared to two people working together toward that goal.

The **crack epidemic destroyed inheritance** before it could even be passed down. **So now, here we are—rebuilding.**

The Reset Starts With You

Understand that when you say **"generational"** (plural), you are making up for a **lost generation.**

But here's the good news—you can **restart the legacy.**

Leave an inheritance but **leave it with instructions.** Teach your kids, educate your family, and seek guidance from professionals on financial planning. There is a wealth of information available for those who were previously locked out or misinformed; this is no longer an excuse. Release the pressure of **making up for lost time**, and instead, **focus on securing the future.** *

Mass incarceration also played a role in wealth destruction, making it impossible for many to obtain life insurance or **find viable employment** to build wealth. But today, **things have changed**. Many offenses can now be **expunged**, and **felons can now obtain life insurance (check with your agent).**

No more excuses. **Leave your family something.** Start the rebuild for real—not just for social media likes.

#Inheritance

UNDERSTANDING WHAT WOMEN TRULY NEED IN A RELATIONSHIP

Relationships have the power to reveal both our strengths and weaknesses. Understanding one another is a crucial part of building a successful relationship, and for men, truly comprehending a woman's needs is essential. The decline in stable family structures has had a profound effect on communities, emphasizing the necessity of strong leadership in the home. While having a father present is valuable, true leadership extends beyond mere presence. To cultivate a strong and enduring relationship, men must actively engage in understanding, communicating, and evolving alongside their partners.

This chapter aims to equip men with the right mindset and tools to build one of the most important yet complex relationships of their lives. Leadership in a relationship is not just about being the decision-maker; it's about making choices that positively impact your partner and family. Often, men will receive blame without praise, both at home and in society. However, remaining strong and resilient, as our forefathers did, is crucial.

Many men have never witnessed a healthy relationship between a man and a woman, particularly if they grew up without a father.

Even those who did may have seen unhealthy dynamics. A long relationship does not necessarily mean a successful one—if there is no emotional or financial growth, no shared vision, or if one partner feels trapped, longevity becomes irrelevant. Healthy relationships require effort, communication, and mutual respect.

While every woman is unique, there are fundamental needs that are often universal: financial and emotional stability, mental wellness protection, love language compatibility, and spiritual recognition. However, these needs are not always expressed in the most direct way, sometimes leaving men feeling as if they're solving a puzzle without all the pieces. This chapter breaks down these concepts to foster deeper understanding and lasting connections.

1. Financial and Emotional Stability: More Than Just Security

Women desire stability beyond material wealth. Financial stability is about responsibility, planning, and security in both good times and bad. Financial decisions can significantly impact a relationship's stability, making open communication about financial goals essential. In my first book, *Christmas is Coming*, I discuss the connection between couples and financial health. A lack of financial trust and planning is a major cause of breakups.

In my previous marriage, financial stability itself was not an issue, but financial discipline was. My ex-wife was not accustomed to financial stability and perceived it as control. I mention this to help men understand that if they enter a relationship with a woman who has never experienced financial stability, they should approach the situation with patience, love, and understanding. It will always be a give and take; remember to always pick your battles.

Equally important is emotional stability, which forms the foundation of a lasting relationship. A woman wants to feel safe in expressing her emotions without fear of being dismissed. Consistency, being reliable, honest, and emotionally available, builds trust. Many men adopt a 'Superman complex,' attempting to fix everything. However, true emotional stability means knowing when to listen rather than trying to provide immediate solutions. This has often been challenging for me because I'm very comical, just part of my nature, not too high, not too low. This can come off as not caring and not being concerned.

2. Mental Wellness Protection vs. Physical Protection

While men have traditionally been seen as physical protectors, modern women seek mental wellness protection. This means fostering an emotionally safe relationship free from toxicity. Listening without immediately trying to fix a problem, acknowledging struggles, and creating a supportive environment are crucial.

Many women carry emotional scars from past relationships, influencing their responses and triggers. Understanding her sensitivities and communicating with care will help create a nurturing relationship rather than an unintentionally harmful one.

3. The Most Common Love Language for Women

Gary Chapman's *The 5 Love Languages* identifies five ways people express and receive love: words of affirmation, quality time, gifts, acts of service, and physical touch. While men often prioritize physical touch, many women resonate with acts of service and words of affirmation.

Love languages require active participation. If a woman says, "I just need you to listen," she often seeks validation, not solutions. Simple acts of service, such as getting her car's oil changed, washing her car, or cooking a meal, can speak volumes. Identifying and consistently applying her love language strengthens the emotional connection. As your relationship evolves, her love language may also shift, which is natural and should be expected. A woman may need more verbal affirmations as she ages and experiences changes in her body, while a younger woman may appreciate thoughtful gifts or small gestures of kindness. However, relying on material expressions of love as a strategy for maintaining a relationship can be unsustainable—if financial challenges arise, true emotional connection and support must take precedence.

4. How Women Communicate: The Unspoken Language

Many men struggle with understanding women because women often communicate in layers, whereas men tend to view things in a more black-and-white manner. Statements like "It's fine" may actually mean "It's not fine, but I don't want to explain it right now." Instead of growing frustrated, men can improve communication by actively listening, asking clarifying questions, and observing behavioral patterns. Women's communication styles require attentiveness and patience. I used to find it humorous how men are expected to intuitively understand what a woman is thinking or what she truly means. Reflecting on my upbringing, I realize my mother did the same thing. I advise against taking every statement literally unless your partner has a strong sense of humor.

Instead of saying, "What do you want me to do?" ask, "Would you like me to help?" This subtle shift reassures her rather than making her feel burdened with decision-making. This doesn't mean you won't sometimes be misunderstood, but the key is persistence. Effective communication requires patience, and the more effort you put into it, the more successful you will be. Often, it helps to rehearse what you want to say in your head to gauge how it sounds and how it may be received.

5. Women's Spiritual Needs

I would like to break this down into 3 parts, as we see the world has forever changed in this area, and those changes may continue. At the end of the day, the question will remain: what do you believe?

Some will say they are not religious but more spiritual, while others trust science over faith and identify as atheists, believing there is no God. I don't judge either way, but it is important to understand where she stands on this matter before becoming deeply involved with her.

A lot of this will be shaped by how she was raised, the beliefs practiced in her home, and her upbringing. As we grow older, we may either adhere to those beliefs or take a strong stance against them. It is imperative to discuss these matters openly, regardless of your personal stance. No matter where you start, I encourage you to grow together rather than compete over who has a better understanding of the belief. Avoid being judgmental—even if you see something you perceive as wrong, remember that leadership applies to all aspects of life, not just selective areas.

In my personal opinion, including God in your relationship can provide guidance and strength when facing challenges. Whatever you do, don't just rely on your own understanding of things.

6. Women's Perspective on Money

For women, financial security is more about responsibility than wealth. Reckless financial behavior is unattractive, while financial planning and ambition are appealing. Often, we assume that women are drawn to flashy displays of wealth—big chains, multiple cars, and extravagant purchases. However, in reality, many women value financial stability, the ability to dress well, enjoy a reliable car, and, most importantly, have a stable home. Owning expensive possessions means little if necessities like shelter and long-term financial security are not met. If you're that guy who hasn't found his financial stride, read my book "Christmas is Coming." Money is the byproduct of responsible behavior.

Men, we often get this wrong, thinking that women want us for our money. They want you because you were designed for her, you are the opposite sex, 2 you should provide for her, not just with money but also with good and sound ideas of what to do with the money,

You may need to take the lead as a responsible steward of finances. A man who lacks financial discipline will face challenges in his relationship, regardless of his income level. I strongly advocate for responsible money management and strategic financial planning. What you don't know can always be learned, so I encourage you to educate yourself on financial decision-making, including investments, to secure a stable future for both you and your partner.

7. The Impact of a Woman Not Growing Up with a Father or Positive Role Model

This is a very serious matter and should not be taken lightly. The first reason is that if you are a father to a little girl, you need to understand the profound impact your presence or absence will have on her adult relationships with men.

That little girl needs to feel validated, loved, and respected for who she is. I have personally witnessed the lasting effects when this does not happen.

In my opinion, women who lack paternal validation may struggle with trust and emotional security. Fathers play a crucial role in shaping their daughters' expectations of men. For men in relationships with women who lacked a father's presence, patience and reassurance are key. I know this personally from raising my bonus daughter from the age of two—she is definitely a daddy's girl. I also contributed to her sister's life, and she is doing amazing things as an adult. I want to personally thank both of their biological dads for trusting me and allowing me to be part of their lives. At some point, I realized I had the ability to give them the confidence that no one else could. Woman will compare what you do to what their fathers did. If dad were present, the pressure would be on my brother. In the same way, if dad or no male role model was present, it is equal or possibly even greater pressure.

Regardless of the situation, you will need to step up to the plate and be the leader she is accustomed to or the one she has never experienced. This will be a blessing to you both and could unlock aspects of her life she has never explored.

I intentionally exposed my bonus daughters to as many experiences as possible, and I continue to do so, ensuring they are not easily impressed by superficial aspects of the world.

Men, let us not take this lightly; it is important to understand the structure of the home your partner grew up in. Some may argue that they did not have their father in the home and turned out fine. While that may be true, I believe that a woman who has not received validation from a respectful and trusted male figure is more likely to struggle in relationships that require male leadership.

8. Woman Saying, "You Are Not a Man"

I had to put this in here; this phrase could wound a man's sense of identity, questioning his ability to lead. Instead of using it as a weapon, women should express concerns in a way that fosters growth rather than tearing down confidence.

A woman could be saying this for many reasons, some but not all including that you are not resembling her father, she could not have ever seen a male and doesn't have a real understanding of what one should be. Recognize the atmosphere when this is said, chances are she is not getting what she wants. I reference this as an adult temper tantrum, like the ones where you would see little kids at the register when they couldn't get that candy. I would walk away and leave you will not win this battle, and an apology will be necessary because you don't want to get into name-calling.

This could be learned behavior, remember most relations take shape around what was in the house growing up. A man's worth is defined by his character and actions, not by a single mistake.

At some point, take the time to understand why she said that. Instead of reacting defensively, reflect on it and acknowledge your emotions. True leadership demands patience, self-awareness, and emotional resilience.

9. Happy Wife, Happy Life: Does the Man Get Less?

We've all heard it countless times — "happy wife, happy life." The idea that the peace and happiness of the household depend solely on her mood. I give two thumbs down to that belief. A successful relationship or marriage requires **mutual fulfillment**, not one-sided satisfaction. If only one partner is happy, the relationship will eventually suffer. True partnership is built on **shared responsibility**, compromise, and the effort to make sure **both individuals feel valued and heard**. Mastering that balance takes time, patience, and commitment to one another. Without it, unresolved issues can build into frustration or emotional distance — leading to survival, not growth.

10. Are Women Really Okay with Being Single for Life?

Many women claim to be content with being single, but for some, this is a defense mechanism against disappointment. The modern woman refuses to settle for less, preferring independence over an unfulfilling relationship. Men should not try to convince a woman she needs a relationship; instead, they should show her how the right relationship enhances her life. My overall opinion is that women are ok with being alone, especially as they get older and have kids or grandchildren to occupy their time.

Women have become strong sources of support for each other, and as a result, they are less likely to tolerate behaviors that do not serve them. Does this mean men are on a short leash? I don't believe so, but it does mean that dishonesty and complacency will not be accepted. Women have made significant strides over the years and now expect men to bring more to the table than just physical intimacy. Most women will tell you that it is not hard to find. The bottom line is that it's time for men to step up, rediscover what makes them desirable, and fulfill the expectations that women rightfully have of them.

Women in the United States gained the right to vote in **1920** with the **19th Amendment** — but in practice, that right largely benefited **white women**. Many **Black women and other women of color** were still blocked from voting through **Jim Crow laws, literacy tests, poll taxes, and intimidation tactics**, especially in the South. It wasn't until the **Voting Rights Act of 1965** that **Black women — and Black men — were truly guaranteed the right to vote** nationwide without discriminatory barriers.

Women were — and still are — paid less than men in most positions. Historically, they were made to feel inferior, often excluded from the workforce, and expected to stay home, cook meals, and raise the children. The old saying *"barefoot and pregnant"* summed up society's expectation of a woman's role. Over time, those shackles began to loosen. Women gained access to education, high-paying jobs, the right to vote, and the freedom to purchase real estate, join the military, and make independent choices. Yet with this progress came a new challenge — what I call a **false sense of independence** that has, in some cases, created division between men and women.

For decades, the narrative was simple: *whoever makes the money is the head of the house.* Traditionally, that was the man. But times have changed. Many women have invested years in education, built careers, and now out-earn their male counterparts. According to the **2024 National Association of REALTORS® Profile of Home Buyers and Sellers, single women accounted for 24% of home purchases**, compared to **11% by single men**. Those numbers raise an uncomfortable question in modern relationships: **If I can do all this on my own — what do I need you for?**

Evenly Yoked

We've all heard the phrase *"be ye not unequally yoked."* It's one of those scriptures often quoted when people talk about relationships, especially within the church. The intention behind it was never wrong—it was meant to protect us from being joined with someone pulling in the opposite direction. The problem is how we've come to understand it. Over time, the phrase became limited to **religious alignment**, as if simply sharing the same faith automatically means two people are equally prepared for partnership.

Many people get lost in that idea—including myself at one point. We assume that because we share the same religious beliefs, we'll also share the same level of spiritual maturity or interpret the Word the same way. That's not always the case. You can attend the same service, read the same scripture, and still live by two very different understandings of what it means.

As I've said before, there may not always be a clear *right* or *wrong*—there's usually a **what works for you** and a **what doesn't**. That's where I want to hang my hat when defining what it really means to be evenly yoked.

The image of being "yoked" comes from farming—two oxen joined together to pull the same load in the same direction. If one moves faster, or one gets distracted, the work becomes unbalanced. Both end up frustrated, even if neither one intended to cause harm. That's what happens in relationships when one person grows while the other stays the same, or when priorities no longer align.

Being evenly yoked isn't about finding someone who just *believes* like you—it's about finding someone who can *build* with you. You can love God, pray daily, and still struggle to love your partner in a healthy way. You can both be spiritual and still unequally yoked in communication, patience, discipline, or forgiveness.

Faith is a foundation, not a finish line. It's a place to start, not a guarantee of harmony. What really matters is whether two people can carry the same weight in the same direction without tearing each other down in the process.

Being evenly yoked means understanding that balance, alignment, and growth matter as much as belief. It means asking:

- Do we interpret love and respect the same way?
- Do we both value growth, accountability, and peace?
- Are we working toward the same vision, even if our paths look different?

That's the part many overlook—the practical side of spiritual connection. It's not just about sharing faith, it's about sharing **function**. You can believe in God and still not be walking toward Him together.

So when I speak about being evenly yoked, I'm not talking about perfection or identical belief systems. I'm talking about two people who move in sync—spiritually, emotionally, and practically. People who understand that being yoked means balance, not bondage. It's not about religion keeping you together—it's about respect, growth, and shared direction keeping you aligned.

Be patient with the process and prepared to do what works. Adjustment is part of alignment. If something stops working, don't force it—fix it. Relationships, like faith, require both grace and maintenance. Being evenly yoked doesn't mean you'll never face friction; it means you'll both be willing to pull together through it.

Personal Perspective: Why I Can Speak on This

Some may question my qualifications to write about women's needs, given that I am not currently married. However, my divorce 18 years ago does not diminish the valuable lessons I have learned about relationships. Instead, it has given me a broader perspective on what nurtures and sustains a healthy partnership. Through years of observation and reflection, I have seen that many married women remain in unfulfilling relationships due to financial stability, children, or fear of the unknown rather than genuine happiness.

Being outside of marriage has given me a unique vantage point, allowing me to analyze relationship dynamics, recognize patterns, and refine my understanding of what makes a lasting partnership work. The insights I share stem from real-life observations, personal growth, and a continuous study of human connection. A thriving marriage isn't merely about coexisting—it's about evolving together, fostering mutual respect, and actively choosing each other every day. My goal is to help both men and women cultivate relationships that are deeply fulfilling, emotionally healthy, and designed to endure life's inevitable ups and downs.

Final Thoughts

Understanding women isn't about mind-reading—it's about presence, active listening, and continuous learning. Relationships require growth, patience, and adaptability. Mutual respect, open communication, and a willingness to evolve together are what create lasting love. The goal is not to "win" her over; it's to build something enduring and meaningful.

Sustaining love requires consistent effort. Here's what men can do:

- **Show up consistently.** Be reliable in both good and challenging times. Your steadiness provides the security she can trust.
- **Adapt to her evolving needs.** A woman's priorities may shift over time. Adjust how you support her as life changes. Growth should happen on both sides.
- **Respect her independence.** Support her ambitions and identity without feeling threatened by them. Her success does not diminish yours—it strengthens the partnership.

And let's be real—as much as we see women enjoying themselves on girls' trips, brunches, and nights out, I still believe that when it's all said and done, most women desire to build a life with a man. There's nothing wrong with sisterhood; connection runs deeper than camaraderie. Prepare yourself for the one who decides to leave the pack—it is what it is, *lol.*

When men commit to understanding and supporting their partners, they build relationships founded on trust, security, and love. True leadership in a relationship isn't about control—it's about **guiding with wisdom, stability, and care.** It's about ensuring that both partners grow together in harmony, not competition.

Love that lasts isn't built on perfection; it's built on two people who keep choosing each other through every season.

PALL BEARER

Growing up in the projects around hundreds of kids, there was always someone you called a friend one week, only to say the next, "You're not my friend anymore." It was almost like a punishment for not getting your way, maybe they refused to share a toy or didn't let you win a game. These moments were part of childhood, an early experience of relationships and boundaries.

As time goes on, friendships form for different reasons. You may have friends from playing on a team, being in an organization, or simply because, out of the mass of people, you connect with a select few and call them friends. But we all know not all friendships are created equally. Some friends you can confide in completely, while others you know to keep at a distance if you don't want your business spread like wildfire. Different types of friendships are okay, and even the strongest ones may weaken over time, just as weaker ones can grow stronger. The key to maintaining friendships is communication and understanding.

Friendships are necessary. I believe deeply in relationships, and I also know they can be extremely complex. How many of us have friendships that exist solely within a specific setting? The work friend you only talk to at work, the club friend who is always down for a night out, or the travel friend who's always ready to book a trip. As life progresses, many things separate us from these friendships. Moving away, getting married, having kids, all of these things change the dynamics of relationships. One of the biggest reasons friendships fade is that you and your friend no longer share the activity that initially brought you together. When that common ground disappears, you must find a new foundation for the relationship, or it will likely drift away.

Gaming and Virtual Friendships

A new way young men are forming friendships is through virtual gaming. They spend hours teaming up, strategizing, and competing against others. This type of connection is often underrated, as it allows individuals to maintain friendships despite changing schools, moving to different states, or other life transitions. Through online gaming, they can stay in contact, exchange numbers, and even meet up in person. However, these friendships come with the same letdowns and expectations as traditional ones, some set times to meet and play, while others may not show up as promised.

While gaming friendships can be valuable, I caution against becoming too dependent on them, as they can create a space of solitude and comfort that may limit real-world social interactions. There is also the inherent risk of not truly knowing who is on the other side of the screen. The younger the gamer, the more important it is to monitor and guide these online connections to ensure they are safe and healthy.

Betrayal and Money in Friendships

Growing apart is normal, but that doesn't mean friendships should be abandoned altogether. True friends share memories, secrets, and experiences that shape who we are. I always question those who don't have any close friends. Who do they talk to? Who do they laugh with? Who do they share life's ups and downs with?

A major test of friendship is **betrayal**. It is often based on an expectation—thinking someone should have done or said something because you would have done it for them. The truth is, we don't always know what influences our friends outside of our presence. Holding grudges over unspoken expectations can lead to unnecessary strain on relationships. Open communication is key.

Another common challenge among friends is **money**. Boy oh boy, this is a big one. My Nana used to say, "Don't borrow money and don't lend money." My PopPop used to say, "Don't lend what you can't afford to lose. Don't lose a friend over $100." Financial misunderstandings have ended countless friendships, not because of the amount borrowed, but because of the unspoken expectations attached to it. If you are going to lend money, be clear about your terms, and if you can afford to, consider giving it as a gift rather than expecting repayment.

Whatever pressure is applied to your friendships, be transparent. Over time, you will learn how to communicate with one another. Some friends are more sensitive than others and understanding how to navigate these differences will help sustain long-term friendships.

Often, men don't express themselves enough for various reasons. Whether due to pride, upbringing, or personal struggles, we tend to internalize emotions rather than talk about them. But friendships thrive on communication. Having friends who understand your struggles and relate to your experiences is invaluable.

A Friend in Need

Don't wait for a friend to reach out to you. Call your friend, visit your friend, and check in if you know or hear they are going through something. Be intentional about your concern for their well-being. Sometimes, people struggle in silence, unsure of how to ask for help. A simple message or visit can mean the world to someone battling hardships. Friendship is not just about the good times.

We all remember the famous words from *New Jack City*: **"Am I my brother's keeper?"** Intervention among men is rare. It seems that women often find more ways to support one another. If you know you have a male friend going through something, intervene. Whether you go alone or bring your crew, get together with him—not just for a day of sports debates, because he may not even be mentally present in that situation. Instead, create a low-volume environment with no outside distractions, free of feminine energy, and talk. Navigate the situation together and let your brother know that he is loved and being thought about. If he doesn't receive it, that's okay—you did your part. Men are meant to be bold, not silent, in these moments. We are to speak up for one another.

Core Friendships

My core group consists of:

- **Fingers** – The youngest of the group, very humble, works hard, and wants the best for everyone.
- **Deuce** – A cool brother, spent a lot of time on road trips together. We have many roommate stories. One of the most intelligent in the crew.
- **Mr. International** – The trendsetter of the crew, enjoys his life without care or concern for outside opinion. A risk-taker through and through.
- **Wood** – Short, bossy, does what he does. Gets along with everybody, never met a stranger.

- **Cheese** – The only child in the crew (no siblings), making his blend unique. Truly enjoys the brotherhood, yet he still values his solitude. Hands down, the meekest of the crew.
- **Alexandro** – The father of the crew. Many, many great moments with this brother. Truly one that belongs in the Hall of Fame of Homies.
- **DJ** – The newest addition to the crew, loves to laugh, is extremely generous, and stays connected in his own way. Currently holds the baby-making record in the crew (he is married).
- **El-Sid** – Protector, overcomer, the true meaning of the word loyal. Consistent, stern, and forgiving at the same time.
- **Bob** – Reminds me of my PopPop—short, another one who never met a stranger. Ten toes down, no filter, and lives life to the fullest as well.
- **Wildgoose** – We don't talk much, but I think of him every day. A wise brother. My island friend, I've known him for over 20 years. His wife and I share the same birthday. We have some of the most candid conversations.
- **Future** — He doesn't just see the future; he *moves toward it.* One of the most creative individuals I've ever met, driven by vision and family. When it comes to surrounding yourself with like-minded people, he's where you start.

The Role of a Pallbearer

The bonds men share throughout life are significant, and ultimately, they are reflected in one of the highest honors of friendship: being a pallbearer. One day, I may have to carry one of these brothers, or one day, they may have to carry me.

Carrying a friend to his final resting place is not just a physical act—it is symbolic of the weight of the memories, the brotherhood, and the shared journey. So, while life changes and friendships evolve, do not take them for granted. Make the call, send the text, check in on your people. Because one day, when the time comes, the strength of those friendships may be measured in who is there to carry you home.

JOINT CUSTODY

When we talk about parenting, especially after a separation or divorce, the word *custody* takes center stage. By definition, **joint custody** refers to a legal arrangement where both parents share decision-making responsibilities and/or physical custody of a child. It means both parents are actively involved in the upbringing of their child, from school choices to medical decisions, from weekend visits to vacations.

There are two main types of joint custody:

- **Joint Legal Custody** – Both parents share the right and responsibility to make decisions concerning the child's upbringing.
- **Joint Physical Custody** – The child spends substantial time living with both parents, though not necessarily equally.

Understanding these terms also means knowing the roles of a **custodial parent** (the one the child lives with most of the time) and a **non-custodial parent** (the one who has visitation rights or shared time but is not the child's primary residence).

This chapter is a message to fathers—especially those navigating the challenges of co-parenting after a breakup. Even when the relationship with the mother is beyond repair, your relationship with your child should never be collateral damage. If you live in the same city or state, **joint custody is one of the most balanced and empowering ways to parent.** It ensures you have a voice in decisions related to schooling, healthcare, extracurriculars, and more.

Don't assume that just because the mother carried the child for nine months, she will automatically make all the right choices or include you in every decision. While many mothers do the right thing, the truth is, not all will. Bitterness, resentment, disagreements over child support, or jealousy over your new relationship can interfere with what's best for the child. That's why having legal rights and responsibilities—*through joint custody*—is so important.

When you have **joint legal and physical custody**, you're not just a weekend dad. You become a consistent presence in your child's life. But that presence also comes with responsibility. For example, if your child stays with you three days a week and the school bus doesn't pick up from your home, you may have to drive them. As the child grows and their needs evolve, flexibility is crucial. If your child builds friendships and wants to ride the bus, you must communicate those changes to the court. Don't assume informal agreements will protect you—because they won't.

Even if things seem amicable now, document everything and follow through legally. If you live out of state or far from your child, make sure your **court order** includes specific holidays and vacation times that you are entitled to. The old mindset of "I don't want to get the courts involved" leaves you vulnerable. Without a court-ordered arrangement, you're at the mercy of the mother's decisions.

When you don't have joint custody—legal or physical—you may have limited access to your child and little say in their life. This can be frustrating and heartbreaking. That's why I urge every man: be intentional, consistent, and proactive. Your presence matters. Your rights matter. And your child deserves the benefit of your love, guidance, and involvement—legally secured and emotionally anchored.

SHARING THE COST

No matter what the custody arrangement looks like, you will be financially responsible for your portion of the child's needs. This includes, but is not limited to, educational materials, medical expenses, daycare, and before or after-school programs. One area that often gets misunderstood or mishandled is **child support**.

Let's be clear: **do not rely on verbal or out-of-court agreements for child support**. Even if you and your child's mother are getting along now, things can change quickly. Any money you provide outside of a legal agreement may be considered a *gift* unless clearly documented, for example, including a memo that states it is for child support. Even then, there's no guarantee it will be recognized in court. Why take the risk? Go to court and get it done the right way. Trust me—this can all go sideways at the most unexpected time.

Now, I'm not saying don't give your child gifts or help out financially beyond what's ordered. Do that—but **do it in addition to** your court-ordered child support, not instead of it. Don't think that, just because you're handing over $50 a week, that you're covering everything. In reality, that amount hardly scratches the surface of what it takes to raise a child today.

The point is: be responsible, be intentional, and get it documented legally. It protects not only you but, more importantly, it ensures your child gets the support they deserve.

NEVER GIVE UP

Just because you do everything you can doesn't always mean it will be enough in the eyes of your child. This is especially true for fathers who are parenting from outside the home. That's the perspective I know all too well, particularly in my relationship with my own son. As children grow, they begin to form their own opinions, values, and social lives—which may at times create distance from your influence or the path you hoped they'd take. These shifts can be challenging and, in some cases, heartbreaking.

Ideally, you and your child's mother are aligned in your co-parenting. If that's the case, it can be easier to address behavior or emotional concerns and develop a plan to help get your child back on track. Open and respectful communication makes a stark difference. But that's the best-case scenario.

In more difficult situations—where you and your co-parent are not on good terms, or where disagreements exist about what's best for your child, you may have to let certain things play out naturally, depending on the child's age and maturity. This can be particularly challenging when children reach their late teens and begin to assert their independence.

In my view, sons especially need to be with their fathers during their teenage years—ideally from around age 13 through high school. If that isn't possible, then it's crucial that they are surrounded by strong, stable male role models. Stability also means consistency in their living environment: minimizing frequent moves or chaotic home situations for at least the next 4–5 years.

In the same way, you may have that daddy's girl who needs just as much attention from her dad as she does from her mom.

For long-distance fathers, the dynamic evolves even more. You may be used to having your child visit during the summer or school breaks, but as they grow older, their social circles, jobs, and extracurricular commitments might make that time more limited. Be prepared for those changes. Instead of insisting on the full summer, be flexible—arrange shorter visits or plan trips to go see them in their environment. Adapt to their changing world without taking it personally.

Parenting from a distance requires patience, creativity, and above all, consistency. Even when your efforts go unnoticed or unreciprocated for a time, keep showing up. Because one day, your child will realize just how much you fought to be present.

THE CHARLIE BROWN EFFECT

It's equally important to incorporate extended family and trusting others into the joint custody experience. Often, when two people break up, the separation extends beyond the couple—it spills over into relationships with each other's family and friends. In some cases, that distance may be necessary for healing. But in most cases, the more loving, consistent support a child receives from both sides of their family, the better off they are.

Let me be clear: just because two parents stay together doesn't mean everything will be smooth and balanced. Dysfunction can exist even in households with both parents present. The goal here is not perfection but collaboration. Having other family members—like grandparents, aunts, uncles, or even close family friends—involved in your child's life gives them additional people to lean on, learn from, and look up to.

There will come a time when your voice, as a parent, starts to sound like noise to your child. The repetition of your rules, reminders, and corrections can wear thin. That's when the support of someone else they trust becomes crucial. You might need to call in an aunt, a mentor, or a family friend to talk through a situation—not to push your agenda, but to offer perspective and help the child process what they're going through.

It takes a village, but it also takes humility. Knowing when to step back and allow others to help guide your child is part of being a great parent. The goal is not control—it's growth, and a healthy community is one of the best tools to support that growth.

PARENTAL FRAUD

Keep in mind, the only reason you are considered a parent is because you have a child. Nothing else qualifies you for that title—not a job, not a pet, not a passion project. In today's world, we hear phrases like "pet parent" or "business baby," but when it comes to raising a real human being, the responsibility is sacred—and real. In this chapter, I want to introduce the concept of what I call **parental fraud**, and more specifically, how some fathers fall into this category.

What does parental fraud look like? It's not about paperwork or legal deception—it's about the **fraud of inaction**. It's being a father in name only, not in practice. It's not showing up for the everyday moments that shape your child's life: the field trips, the spelling bees, the parent-teacher conferences, the weekend games. It's failing to be consistent, creative, and intentional in your involvement. If you're only showing up when it's convenient or when there's praise to be had, you're committing fraud against the child who carries your name.

Being a parent is not a temporary title—it doesn't expire when your child turns 18. In fact, parenting often becomes more emotionally complex as they grow into adulthood. Think back to when you turned 18. Did you have it all figured out? Most of us didn't—and our children won't either. That's why your continued presence matters. Guidance, support, and consistent connection are needed well beyond the teenage years.

You may have to make sacrifices—some decisions won't be easy or desirable. But the long-term investment pays off in the strength of the bond you build. As a father, you set the tone. You are the walking blueprint for how your child will engage with the world, resolve conflict, and treat others.

Encourage your children to respect their other parent. Never use them as pawns in adult disputes and never celebrate conflict with your co-parent. Children watch, absorb, and internalize more than we realize. As a man, your leadership should be grounded in maturity, humility, and a commitment to your child's full well-being.

And to be fair, although this book focuses on manhood and fatherhood, there are also mothers who commit parental fraud. Some use custody as control, some neglect the emotional and physical needs of the child, and some put their own bitterness above the child's growth. No parent—mother or father—should take the title if they are not willing to carry the responsibility.

Parental fraud is not just a failure to act; it's a failure to care, to engage, and to lead. And if you're reading this, it's not too late to correct that. Show up. Stay consistent. Be the parent your child deserves.

STAND YOUR GROUND

Being a parent in a joint custody situation can be extremely challenging—but let me encourage you by saying that it's absolutely possible to be successful. You may not always be liked. Friends and even family might disagree with your decisions, some of which may be made in your child's best interest but misunderstood by others. In fact, some of those decisions might even put you at odds with your own child. But stand firm.

This book was born from a real decision I had to make—to relocate and be closer to my child after his mother and I divorced. It was not an easy choice. And let me be honest: there were moments when I felt completely unsupported, even by those closest to me. This kind of lack of support isn't the same as people simply disagreeing with you—it's deeper. It's when people don't believe in your mission, your role, or your willingness to do what's necessary for your child's well-being.

That's why it's critical to pray about every major decision you face. Don't rush the process. Consult those who've walked a similar path. Pay attention to the history between you, your child, and your co-parent. The insight you need might come from someone who's already been where you are.

Whether you're living in the home or parenting from a distance, you'll face tough financial and emotional decisions. Your children may still need help after they turn 18, perhaps you've already helped pay for college, bought them a car, or supported them through a difficult time. But eventually, there needs to be a clear line drawn. You must discern when support turns into enabling. They need to learn how to grow—not just rely.

That brings me to a hard reality: adult children still living at home in their 30s, 40s, or 50s. Society may say that's too old, and maybe in many cases, it is. The real question is, are they making progress? If they're living with you, ask yourself—if something happened to you tomorrow, would they be able to survive on their own? Would they know how to pay bills, keep a job, or navigate life's responsibilities? If the answer is no, you may need to have the uncomfortable conversation and set a clear plan.

Help your children transition from dependency to independence. Set timelines. Teach them life skills. Don't just house them, prepare them.

And yes, sometimes that means asking them to leave. If they can't respect your home, your rules, your boundaries, then you may have to make that tough decision. Whether it's about staying out too late, bringing the wrong energy into your space, or simply refusing to grow up, you cannot let your home become a shelter for stagnation.

As the father—the man—you will often be the one called to make those hard choices. So, make them. Stand your ground, set the plan, and follow through.

Just do it.

Joint Custody

When we talk about parenting, especially after a separation or divorce, the word *custody* takes center stage. By definition, **joint custody** refers to a legal arrangement where both parents share decision-making responsibilities and/or physical custody of a child. It means both parents are actively involved in the upbringing of their child, from school choices to medical decisions, from weekend visits to vacations.

There are two main types of joint custody:

- **Joint Legal Custody** – Both parents share the right and responsibility to make decisions concerning the child's upbringing.

- **Joint Physical Custody** – The child spends substantial time living with both parents, though not necessarily equally.

Understanding these terms also means knowing the roles of a **custodial parent** (the one the child lives with most of the time) and a **non-custodial parent** (the one who has visitation rights or shared time but is not the child's primary residence).

This chapter is a message to fathers—especially those navigating the challenges of co-parenting after a breakup. Even when the relationship with the mother is beyond repair, your relationship with your child should never be collateral damage. If you live in the same city or state, **joint custody is one of the most balanced and empowering ways to parent.** It ensures you have a voice in decisions related to schooling, healthcare, extracurriculars, and more.

Don't assume that just because the mother carried the child for nine months, she will automatically make all the right choices or include you in every decision. While many mothers do the right thing, the truth is, not all will. Bitterness, resentment, disagreements over child support, or jealousy over your new relationship can interfere with what's best for the child. That's why having legal rights and responsibilities—*through joint custody*—is so important.

When you have **joint legal and physical custody**, you're not just a weekend dad. You become a consistent presence in your child's life. But that presence also comes with responsibility. For example, if your child stays with you three days a week and the school bus doesn't pick up from your home, you may have to drive them. As the child grows and their needs evolve, flexibility is crucial. If your child builds friendships and wants to ride the bus, you must communicate those changes to the court. Don't assume informal agreements will protect you—because they won't.

Even if things seem amicable now, document everything and follow through legally. If you live out of state or far from your child, make sure your **court order** includes specific holidays and vacation times that you are entitled to. The old mindset of "I don't want to get the courts involved" leaves you vulnerable. Without a court-ordered arrangement, you're at the mercy of the mother's decisions.

When you don't have joint custody—legal or physical—you may have limited access to your child and little say in their life. This can be frustrating and heartbreaking. That's why I urge every man: be intentional, consistent, and proactive. Your presence matters. Your rights matter. And your child deserves the benefit of your love, guidance, and involvement—legally secured and emotionally anchored.

FACING HARD DECISIONS

Being a parent in a joint custody situation can be extremely challenging—but let me encourage you by saying that it's absolutely possible to be successful. You may not always be liked. Friends and even family might disagree with your decisions, some of which may be made in your child's best interest but misunderstood by others. In fact, some of those decisions might even put you at odds with your own child. But stand firm.

This book was born from a real decision I had to make—to relocate and be closer to my child after his mother and I divorced. It was not an easy choice. And let me be honest: there were moments when I felt completely unsupported, even by those closest to me. This kind of lack of support isn't the same as people simply disagreeing with you—it's deeper. It's when people don't believe in your mission, your role, or your willingness to do what's necessary for your child's well-being.

That's why it's critical to pray about every major decision you face. Don't rush the process. Consult those who've walked a similar path. Pay attention to the history between you, your child, and your co-parent. The insight you need might come from someone who's already been where you are.

Whether you're living in the home or parenting from a distance, you'll face tough financial and emotional decisions. Your children may still need help after they turn 18, perhaps you've already helped pay for college, bought them a car, or supported them through a difficult time. But eventually, there needs to be a clear line drawn. You must discern when support turns into enabling. They need to learn how to grow—not just rely.

That brings me to a hard reality: adult children still living at home in their 30s, 40s, or 50s. Society may say that's too old, and maybe in many cases, they are. The real question is, are they making progress? If they're living with you, ask yourself—if something happened to you tomorrow, would they be able to survive on their own? Would they know how to pay bills, keep a job, or navigate life's responsibilities? If the answer is no, you may need to have the uncomfortable conversation and set a clear plan.

Help your children transition from dependency to independence. Set timelines. Teach them life skills. Don't just house them, prepare them.

And yes, sometimes that means asking them to leave. If they can't respect your home, your rules, your boundaries, then you may have to make that tough decision. Whether it's about staying out too late, bringing the wrong energy into your space, or simply refusing to grow up, you cannot let your home become a shelter for stagnation.

As the father—the man—you will often be the one called to make those hard choices. So, make them. Stand your ground, set the plan, and follow through.

Just do it.

THEN THIS HAPPENED

Life is full of unexpected moments—some that change the course of your path entirely and others that serve as lessons along the way. Sometimes, you prepare for an outcome, only to find yourself facing a completely different reality. Other times, an event sneaks up on you without warning, forcing you to adapt, rebuild, and move forward.

Just a week before my grandmother's birthday she was hospitalized, ultimately never to leave the hospital alive. I was preparing to go to CT to celebrate her 97 Birthday. It may have been a then this happened moment for her as well. I recall having a conversation with her when she was 90, I asked her the question now what Nana, you made it to 90, her response was I want to live as long as my daddy, he died at 97. Just 3 days before her 97th Birthday she passed away.

Of course, I can go on to many more of these unexpected unplanned moments in life but for this chapter, I want to speak about becoming a Bonus dad, something I had never planned for. Many men find themselves in similar situations, unexpectedly stepping into the role of a father figure for a child who looks to them for guidance and security.

I found myself in a relationship with a woman who had two daughters. The youngest was two years old, and the oldest was six. The older daughter had a good relationship with her father, but the little one hadn't yet formed that bond. As a result, she started calling me "Daddy." I believe she thought that was my name—after all, my son who was about the same age was calling me that, so she followed along. Without fully understanding the weight of the title, she innocently looked to me for direction and instruction, as all children do. Just like that, I found myself in a role I had never planned for. Now some may ask the question or make an obvious observation of me knowing she had children before dating her. That would be an accurate observation, and I did she didn't and obviously couldn't hide that. In just because you get into that situation what I want to go a little deeper with is the role in it.

Surely you may face backlash from your previous relationship being accused of treating your bonus children better than your biological ones. If this is true, I encourage you to find a way to balance the two although you didn't plan for this it happened now, and situations are not an excuse for lack of responsibility. On the other hand, if this is not the case move on and be mindful of the resistance you have to her until your child becomes of age if they are not already. Utilize the court to make sure you have visitation rights; resistance is no excuse for not seeing your child. Don't be surprised to hear a woman say, I don't want my kids around her, or I don't know her. Now this may be a genuine concern for an infant or small child, be as transparent as you possibly can but ultimately maintain the relationship with your biological child(children).

After many conversations with friends who had been in similar situations, I'm reminded of what my cousin Larry once said: "If you feed her, that's your child." You see Larry had married a woman that had a child already so speaking to him I knew he could give me some good advice. His daughter Jasmine was a beautiful soul and undoubtedly made it easy for Larry to reply to my question. Even after hearing that, I wasn't sure if this was for me. It wasn't about the present role I had to play—it was about the long haul. I questioned whether it was fair to Anaya if her mother and I didn't work out and she grew attached to me. With my biological son, there would always be legal recognition and an ongoing connection, but with her, it would be different. If we parted ways, she would be left with only feelings and memories. Because of that, I resisted fully embracing the role in my own mind.

But resistance became difficult. She was a sweet and respectful little girl, and due to her mother's schedule, I spent a lot of time with both kids. She quickly became attached to me, and I could feel her trust growing—whether it was carrying her to bed after she fell asleep in the car, reaching her arms up for me to pick her up, or rushing to the door every time I picked up my keys. I realized then that if I was going to be in her life, I needed to be present in full—not just for her mother, but for her as well. Many refer to it as a package deal.

For any man in this situation, I encourage you to do the upright thing. Don't just be there for the mother and avoid engaging with the children. If you're in their lives, you are a role model, whether you realize it or not. They need your presence, consistency, and guidance. Be mindful of what you say and how you act around them. Discipline them with love, just as you would your own children. Often times Anaya would run to her mom telling her what I said or did, especially when it was a no, you can't go, or no, you can't have that right now. What was good is her mom would say, well, if that's what he said, that's what it is, well, 90% of the time she would. Positive reinforcement is necessary to have the type of relationship I'm talking about, so if you're a mom and you're reading this, allow the man that you decided was good enough to be around your kids to discipline them as well. Now I'm not condoning hitting or name-calling calling as I have seen in a few relationships, this can harm the child, and the relationship between mom and children.

As I embraced the role, I found myself doing things I had never imagined—like doing her hair in the mornings before school. I remember her teachers saying, "Looks like your dad did your hair today," only for me to pick her up with a different hairstyle altogether. It was in the small, everyday moments that I realized how much of an impact I was making. Taking her to salons to get her hair done or asking a random woman to take her to the bathroom.

The thing that drew me in was watching the bond between my son, Duncan, and Anaya. They were just innocent kids enjoying each other's company, playing together for hours, making jokes, and sharing laughter. Celebrating each other's birthdays together, and many other special occasions like Duncan's soccer games, doing karate together, and showing support for one another. Those moments made me realize that love isn't limited to biological ties. Loving a child who isn't biologically yours is a different kind of experience—one that requires intention and commitment.

As Anaya grew older, she continued to call me "Dad" not just as a name but as an acknowledgment of my role in her life. I would visit her school for lunch and attend her field trips and events. I remember hearing her friends ask, "Anaya, is that your dad?" She would smile, move closer to me, and say, "Yes."

At first glance, people wouldn't assume I was her dad. I am a dark-skinned man, and she is noticeably light. Although it never happened, I always thought someone might call the police, thinking she was in danger. But every time, her smile reassured them that everything was just as it should be.

Stepping into this role was never in my plans, but it became one of the most meaningful experiences of my life.

As time passed, Anaya's biological father began to come back into her life. While she initially resisted it, I encouraged her to embrace the relationship. I knew my role, and I was never fearful that one day she would forget or become ungrateful. That is not the mindset a parent or role model should have. do it with no expectation of praise or return. I reassured her, "Anaya, some kids don't even have one dad, but you have two."

As she matured, she came to appreciate this perspective. I continued to encourage her to visit him, to allow herself to feel her emotions, but to never hold onto anger. I told her, "We all make mistakes, and forgiveness is something you can learn and grow from." Over time, she embraced her relationship with both of us, understanding that love is not divided but multiplied.

One of the most memorable moments was when she got ready for her prom. Her biological father and I stood on either side of her, and got some pictures, both of us showing our support and love for the amazing young woman she had become. That moment was a testament to what happens when men put their pride aside for a greater purpose—one common love, Anaya. If you happen to be the man in the position her father was in, I encourage you to embrace your faults or missed opportunities for whatever reason. You can still be a healthy part of your child's life as you should for the sake of the child get along chances are it's only on special days in their life like graduations, proms, birthdays, etc.

Message to Anaya

Anaya, you have taught me more than I have probably taught you, and I thank you for that. Throughout the tough times in my life, you always smiled at me and kept your confidence in me. What a wonderful time we had at the daddy-daughter dance, and on so many long trips where you and Duncan would lean on each other to fall asleep in the backseat. You were then and still are so possessive of me being your dad, it makes you happy as you have told me so many times over.

I'm sure there are things in your life you feel you will never speak to me about, and I understand—there are things in my life I'll never speak to my mom about or Grammy, as you call her, and as she recently told me you have been calling her Queen grammy. Just know, I'm a dad, a lot of things you don't have to say, I already know. I encourage you to find your way in all phases of your life. Yes, my dear, life has many phases. You've gone through a few, and you have many more to go. Don't fear them, rather embrace them and enjoy the growth and the opportunity that life brings. Like the opportunity I was given to be in your life once I embraced it and started to enjoy it, this is the result. Stay close to your family, and always encourage your friends, because one day, they may need to encourage you.

As a young lady, I know you want to always do what is right, but that phase of your life is over. Now, you must do what works for you, not what I think you should do. We have been tested before, so you know I will never turn my back on you, even though there are things I don't like or wouldn't choose for you. In the process, stop and evaluate your progress or the lack of progress. Don't beat yourself up if something you attempted to do didn't work or is not working; make the appropriate changes and learn from it.

One day, you will be a mom, although you say no, and one day, you will have to choose a young man to court—someone that you love. I caution you not to look for me in him but know that my treatment of you is unique. God knew what you needed, and He sent me. In the same way, he knew what I needed and sent you. There will come a time when that same God sees what you need and sends someone to spend the rest of your life with.

Just know I'll be there for all the things you may not understand about guys, and we can do what we always do, have a long talk and laugh about it while ignoring all the calls coming in. Until, of course, Loren calls…

Keep your friends. You both will grow and become more involved in your own lives, but don't feel like they are leaving you if this happens. Make time for each other, even if it means traveling to spend a weekend together. It will be worth it when you all have careers and families and look back on your younger days.

I couldn't write a message to you without telling you to save your money and read my book for a good financial plan. If ever you feel life is getting the best of you, seek counsel if you need to, no matter what phase of life you're in.

Include God in everything you do; without him, there is no me and you. He gave me the strength to do what I didn't know I could. He will give you the same strength in your times of weakness and uncertainty.

Keep effective communication with your siblings, including Duncan. You both recognize each other as family, so be there for each other as life goes on—sometimes, that may be the only support you have. Share pictures, as you have many to share and talk about the foundation that was set for you all.

One day, my audible voice and physical presence will no longer exist, so I write this message to you so that you will forever hear it in the earlobes of your heart. "Then this happened" moments often reshape us in ways we never expected. It's what we choose to do with those moments that defines the individuals we become.

Message to Jenaya

I can honestly say that as a parent, I never expect anything in return. I'll never forget that one day, for my birthday, you gave me a bag full of the things you knew I liked — a Panthers hat and some cologne. If I told you I didn't shed a tear, I'd be lying. Your thoughtfulness is infectious and never goes unnoticed.

What a day it was when you called to tell me you were coming to Charlotte to attend school. I can still remember the excitement in your voice — that mix of courage, determination, and nervousness. You were stepping into a new city, chasing your goals, and doing it all with the confidence of someone who already knew she'd make it.

Watching you graduate and step right into the workforce was one of those proud-father moments I'll never forget. It reminded me that everything I've ever said to you — every lesson, every talk, every challenge — had taken root. You listened, and you applied it.

Long before that, I remember you as that little girl on the sidelines, pom-poms in hand, smiling brighter than anyone else on the field. Cheerleading wasn't just something you did — it was something that showed who you were. You had energy, spirit, and the ability to lift people up, even when you didn't realize it. Whether you were performing in front of a crowd or just being yourself at home, your light always filled the room.

Nothing you do surprises me, because you've always had a way of balancing everything that mattered — being a big sister, keeping good grades, and managing work or school, often both at the same time. You've always known how to handle your business and stay focused on what really matters. I've seen you laugh and I've seen you cry, yet through it all, you've moved forward with strength and grace. You don't get easily distracted by the noise that surrounds so many people today — the pull of social media, the influence of peers, or the weight of gossip. You've stayed grounded, steady, and real. That's rare — and it's something I deeply admire about you.

One of your most mature qualities is your ability to take correction and seek advice when you know you need it, even though, most of the time, you already know what I'm going to say. That's what growth looks like — knowing how to pause, think, and make wise choices, even when emotions are high or the road gets uncertain.

You're also blessed to have **two dads** who love you in their own ways — each of us wanting the best for you, each proud of the woman you've become. Not every child experiences that kind of double portion of love and guidance, and I'm grateful that you've always managed to honor both relationships with maturity and understanding.

And while I'm not your biological father, you've allowed me to step into a space that many men never get the chance to fill — a place of guidance, trust, and respect. You've allowed me to give advice when you needed it and to simply listen when words weren't enough. As a stepdad, one of the hardest things you can ever hear is, "You're not my dad." But you never said that. You allowed me to be present, to help, to guide, and to love you in the way I knew how. That alone means more than I could ever express.

Through all of life's seasons, you've continued to shine with grace, humility, and quiet strength. You've faced challenges that would have broken many, yet you handled them with balance and faith. You've shown me what it means to be resilient, to adapt, and to keep your light steady even when the world tries to dim it.

I've always told you that life is about progress, not perfection. Watching you evolve has reminded me that our children often become our greatest teachers. You've taught me patience, compassion, and the beauty of letting go while still being present.

Thank you for allowing me to be part of all your greatest moments — and for the privilege of watching you step into womanhood with confidence and purpose. I look forward to every new chapter of your journey.

You've made me proud not just because of what you've accomplished, but because of who you've become.

Keep leading with love and keep living with intention.

I AM

The Power of Identity and Self-Talk

"I Am" is a state of being. The words we use to define ourselves shape our identity, influence our actions, and determine how we navigate life. It's important to be mindful of who we tell ourselves we are. Just because you have made a mistake does not mean you are that mistake. Committing a crime does not mean you are inherently a criminal, and having a felony does not mean you are defined by it. Labels can be dangerous when we accept them as truth, especially when they come from a place of negativity or condemnation.

It's not just about the words others use to define us; it's also about the words we use to define ourselves. Be mindful of the negative things you allow people to call you. I'm not saying you need to defend yourself verbally or physically, but the old saying "sticks and stones may break my bones, but words will never hurt me" is simply not true. Many altercations have started over words alone. As kids, we used to joke and roast each other all the time, myself included. What I learned is that while some kids could handle it, others could not—and regardless, it was not okay. As adults, name-calling is no longer acceptable and, in some cases, can have dire consequences.

Even more importantly, be mindful of the things you tell yourself. Self-perception is powerful—if you consistently define yourself by your past, shortcomings, or mistakes, you reinforce a mindset that limits your potential.

The Impact of Words

As children, many of us were conditioned to reinforce negative self-perceptions without even realizing it. I remember hearing parents tell their kids, "Say you're sorry." The child, most likely with their head down, would mumble, "I'm sorry." In some cases, the parent would respond, "I didn't hear you," forcing the child to repeat the words again, further instilling a sense of personal shame. Over time, constantly saying, "I'm sorry," can turn into an identity rather than an acknowledgment of a single action.

This is not about denying responsibility or avoiding accountability, it is about speaking with intention. Rather than saying, "I'm sorry," consider saying, "I apologize for…" and clearly state what you are apologizing for. This small shift helps separate the act from the identity. You are not a sorry person; you are someone who recognizes a mistake and makes amends.

Affirming Who You Are

Back in 1997, when I became a real estate agent, one of our exercises was cold calling—calling through a list of contacts and reciting a script to see if they had any real estate needs. Before making calls, we practiced a series of affirmations to build our confidence, preparing ourselves to handle rejection. Another requirement was to have a mirror at our desk and stand up while speaking on the phone, ensuring we projected confidence and maintained a positive mindset. This practice was invaluable to me and remains beneficial even today.

The way you define yourself sets the tone for your life. Instead of reinforcing negative labels, it's essential to adopt positive affirmations that align with who you truly are and who you strive to become. I am currently a mentor in a youth program, and one of the most impactful things we do at the beginning of each class is recite the following affirmation:

I am POWERFUL

I am RESPECTFUL

I am OPTIMISTIC

I MAKE good decisions

I am INTELLIGENT

I am STRONG and

EVERYTHING I do matters

This powerful affirmation was created by Tesha Boyd of "Promise Youth Development." Week after week, kids of all ages recite and internalize it. Just as constantly saying "I am sorry" can shape self-perception, repeating positive affirmations helps build confidence and a strong sense of identity.

- **I am strong.**
- **I am capable.**
- **I am resilient.**
- **I am learning and growing.**
- **I am not my past mistakes.**
- **I am becoming the best version of myself.**

By practicing positive self-talk, you take control of your identity and reshape your narrative. The goal is not to ignore reality, but to recognize that you are more than any one moment, decision, or label that has been placed upon you.

Choosing Your Own Identity

We all have the power to redefine ourselves. The key is being intentional about what we choose to accept and reject. Every day, we have the opportunity to affirm who we are and take steps toward who we want to become. Be mindful of what follows your "I Am." Make sure it reflects not just where you've been, but where you are going.

POLITICAL PILL

Political Pulp

Politics is one of the most divisive topics in modern society. Whether at the dinner table, the workplace, or online, political discussions can quickly escalate into heated debates. Especially with my brother, Derrick he and I have healthy debates often, sharing links to further support our belief on a particular topic. When I became a real estate agent, I was advised to stay away from two topics the first was religion and the other was politics. As men, understanding politics isn't just about choosing sides—it's about being informed, aware, and prepared for how policies and decisions affect our lives, families, and futures. This chapter is not meant to turn men into politicians but to provide awareness of the system that governs us all.

Political Colors and Labels

In American politics, colors and labels play a significant role in defining ideologies and party affiliations. The most common representations are:

- **Red (Republican)** – Typically associated with conservatism, which values tradition, limited government intervention, free-market capitalism, and strong national defense.

- **Blue (Democrat)** – Represents progressiveness, which supports social change, government programs to aid citizens, and policies that promote equality and diversity.

- **Left vs. Right** – The "left" generally refers to liberal, progressive ideals, while the "right" aligns with conservative, traditional values. The degree to which a person identifies with either side can range from moderate to extreme.

- **Independent/Third Party** – Some individuals and groups do not fully align with either major party and support independent or third-party candidates.

Understanding these labels is crucial because they often shape how people perceive policies, leadership, and societal issues. Many individuals develop political allegiances based on family tradition, ethnic background, or even the influence of their spouse. While these factors can shape viewpoints, it's important to recognize that political beliefs are complex and should be formed through personal understanding, research, and reflection rather than blind loyalty to a particular party.

The Role of Men in Politics

Historically, political leadership in the U.S. has been dominated by men. Every president in American history has been male. However, two women—Hillary Clinton, wife of former President Bill Clinton, and Kamala Harris—have reached historic milestones, both representing the Democratic Party. Clinton was the first female presidential nominee of a major political party in 2016, while Kamala Harris made history as the first Black Vice President and the first female Vice President of the United States. Though Harris never secured a presidential nomination, her rise to the second-highest office in the nation marked a significant moment in political history. Kamala also ran in the 2024 election for president after Joseph Biden stepped down due to health concerns, making her another historic candidate for the presidency.

Men have long been at the forefront of shaping political policies, laws, and decisions. One of the most historic milestones in American politics was the election of **Barack Obama**, the first Black president of the United States. His presidency, spanning from 2009 to 2017, was a significant moment in history, breaking racial barriers in a role that had been exclusively held by white men for over two centuries. His election demonstrated a shift in the political landscape and reflected the growing diversity of leadership in the country.

Another unique presidency was that of **Donald Trump**, who survived an assassination attempt during the 2024 presidential campaign. On July 13, 2024, at a rally in Butler, Pennsylvania, a gunman fired multiple shots, with one bullet grazing Trump's upper right ear. The shooter, identified as Thomas Matthew Crooks, was neutralized by the Secret Service, but the incident resulted in casualties among attendees. This attack highlighted security concerns for political figures and added to the contentious nature of the election (en.wikipedia.org, nypost.com).

Trump went on to achieve a notable victory in the 2024 U.S. presidential election, securing 312 electoral votes to Kamala Harris's 226 (en.wikipedia.org). He also won the popular vote, obtaining 49.8% compared to Harris's 48.3% (en.wikipedia.org). This made Trump the second president in U.S. history, after Grover Cleveland, to serve non-consecutive terms.

Trump's re-election was part of a global backlash against incumbent parties, influenced by factors such as the 2021–2023 inflation surge (en.wikipedia.org). His victory was described as an extraordinary comeback for a former president (pbs.org).

The election results were officially certified by Congress on January 6, 2025, with Vice President Kamala Harris presiding over the proceedings (cnn.com). This certification process was notably peaceful, contrasting with the events following the 2020 election (aljazeera.com).

Trump's inauguration marked a significant moment in U.S. political history, as he became the first president to return to office after a defeat since Cleveland in 1893 (en.wikipedia.org)., He achieved a notable victory in the 2024 U.S. presidential election, securing 312 electoral votes to Kamala Harris's 226 (en.wikipedia.org). He also won the popular vote, obtaining 49.8% compared to Harris's 48.3% (en.wikipedia.org). This made Trump the second president in U.S. history, after Grover Cleveland, to serve non-consecutive terms.

Trump's re-election was part of a global backlash against incumbent parties, influenced by factors such as the 2021–2023 inflation surge (en.wikipedia.org). His victory was described as an extraordinary comeback for a former president (pbs.org).

The election results were officially certified by Congress on January 6, 2025, with Vice President Kamala Harris presiding over the proceedings (cnn.com). This certification process was notably peaceful, contrasting with the events following the 2020 election (aljazeera.com).

Trump's inauguration marked a significant moment in U.S. political history, as he became the first president to return to office after a defeat since Cleveland in 1893 (en.wikipedia.org)., a businessman with no prior political experience who disrupted traditional political norms. His election in 2016 highlighted the growing frustration with career politicians and showcased how an outsider could ascend to the highest office in the country. While Trump's presidency was filled with controversy, from policy decisions to impeachment trials, his approach demonstrated the influence of business acumen in politics. Though he was the first businessman to successfully win the presidency, others like Ross Perot had previously run, indicating that unconventional candidates could challenge the status quo and gain significant support. His election demonstrated a shift in the political landscape and reflected the growing diversity of leadership in the country. Whether by design or historical circumstances, politics has traditionally been a male-dominated field. This makes it even more important for men today to be politically aware, regardless of their party affiliation.

Understanding Government: The House, Senate, Congress, and Supreme Court

The **Supreme Court** is the highest judicial authority in the United States. It plays a critical role in interpreting the Constitution, reviewing laws, and making decisions that shape the nation's legal landscape. The Court consists of nine Justices—one Chief Justice and eight Associate Justices—who are appointed by the President and confirmed by the Senate. These Justices serve lifetime appointments, ensuring their decisions remain independent of political pressure.

The Supreme Court has the power of **judicial review**, meaning it can strike down laws or executive actions that are deemed unconstitutional. Major historical rulings have shaped civil rights, personal freedoms, and government policies, making the Court one of the most influential institutions in the country.

While many focus on the President and Congress when discussing political power, the Supreme Court's rulings often have lasting impacts on American society. Understanding its role is crucial to grasping the full scope of how the U.S. government functions.

The U.S. government operates under a system of checks and balances designed to distribute power among different branches. Within the legislative branch, there are three key components:

- **House of Representatives** – Members (called Representatives) are elected based on state population. Larger states have more representatives than smaller ones. They serve two-year terms and are responsible for introducing and voting on laws.

- **Senate** – Each state has two Senators, regardless of size, serving six-year terms. The Senate reviews and votes on laws, confirms presidential appointments, and has the power to conduct impeachment trials.

- **Congress** – This refers to both the House and Senate together. Congress is responsible for making laws, approving budgets, and overseeing government operations.

Understanding these roles is essential to recognizing how laws are passed and who is responsible for making decisions that impact daily life.

How Laws and Policies Are Made

Laws in the U.S. go through a rigorous process before being enacted:

1. **Introduction** – A bill is proposed in either the House or the Senate.
2. **Committee Review** – The bill is sent to a committee that examines and revises it.
3. **Debate and Vote** – The bill is debated and voted on in the House and Senate.
4. **Presidential Approval** – If both chambers pass the bill, it goes to the president for approval or veto.
5. **Becoming Law** – If signed by the president, the bill becomes law. If vetoed, Congress can override the veto with a two-thirds majority vote.

Federal vs. State Government

One of the biggest misunderstandings in politics is the difference between federal and state power. The U.S. operates under a dual system where:

- **Federal Government** – Handles national issues like defense, foreign policy, and federal laws that apply to all states.
- **State Government** – Controls local matters like education, policing, and state-specific laws. Each state has its own constitution and government structure.

This distinction is important because many policies affecting daily life—such as taxes, gun laws, and healthcare—are determined at the state level rather than federally.

Political Influence

Politics is not just about laws and policies—it's also about influence. One of the biggest influencers in modern politics is the media. Different news outlets cater to specific political parties, shaping the way people perceive events and policies. Understanding media bias is crucial for any man who wants to be informed rather than manipulated.

Some major news networks lean toward one party or ideology:

- **Left-Leaning (Liberal/Progressive)** – Outlets like CNN, MSNBC, and The New York Times tend to support Democratic policies and progressive ideals.
- **Right-Leaning (Conservative)** – Fox News, The Wall Street Journal (editorial section), and Newsmax often align with Republican perspectives.
- **Moderate or Independent** – Some outlets, like Reuters and The Associated Press, aim to provide neutral coverage, though biases can still exist.
- **New Media-**Let us not forget the so-called new media, consisting of podcasts and other journalists who have been let go of major networks and started their own followings on YouTube and social media.

The key to being politically aware is exploring multiple sources and cross-referencing information. Don't rely solely on one news outlet. Instead, read from different perspectives to get the best and most balanced understanding of an issue.

Influence of Entertainers in Politics

Beyond traditional media, politicians often use entertainers, including sports figures, actors, and music artists, to sway public opinion. These public figures have a massive reach, and their endorsements can influence people who may not have been previously interested in politics. Whether through campaign ads, social media posts, or event appearances, entertainers help drive political narratives and mobilize voters.

However, it's important not to be fooled by celebrity endorsements. Many entertainers are compensated for their participation in political campaigns, and their personal interests may not align with those of the general public. Before allowing a celebrity's opinion to shape your vote, ask yourself: *What do I have in common with this person? Do they truly represent my values and concerns, or do they simply play a role in a political agenda?* Critical thinking and independent research are key to avoiding blind allegiance based on star power alone.

The Role of Division in Politics

Politics doesn't just shape policies—it also shapes relationships. Political views have become so polarizing that they often divide families, friendships, and entire communities. Something as simple as a bumper sticker, a yard sign, or a social media post can spark heated debates, creating rifts between people who otherwise share common interests. The ongoing debate between "red versus blue" has turned into an endless cycle of conflict, making it harder for individuals to have open, respectful discussions.

Instead of getting caught up in political arguments that strain relationships, some choose to keep their views private, understanding that these debates rarely lead to meaningful change at the personal level. Being aware of the political climate in both your home state and the places you travel to is also important, as laws, policies, and even social expectations vary widely across different regions.

Political leaders and media outlets often use division as a tool to rally support. One of the most common strategies is using race, economic class, and social status to pit groups against each other. For example:

- **Race and Politics** – Political parties sometimes appeal to racial identity to gain votes, often framing issues as "us versus them."

- **Economic Division** – There is constant rhetoric about the middle class versus the upper class or billionaires. Some argue that the rich don't pay enough taxes, while others believe they are job creators who should not be over-taxed. This division creates tension and fuels resentment among economic classes.

Understanding these tactics helps men recognize when they are being influenced emotionally rather than logically. Staying informed and thinking critically about policies—rather than reacting emotionally to party-driven narratives—can prevent falling into these political traps.

Local Government and Its Structure

While national politics gets the most attention, local government has a direct impact on daily life. Understanding how local leadership is structured is just as important as knowing what happens in Washington, D.C.

- **District Representatives** – Each city and county is divided into districts, with elected officials representing local communities. These officials influence city planning, education, and local policies.

- **State Legislature** – Each state has its own House and Senate, which create and vote on state laws. State legislatures handle issues like taxes, education funding, and infrastructure.

- **Governor** – The governor is the leader of a state, similar to how the president leads the country. Governors approve or veto state laws, manage state budgets, and oversee emergency responses.

Many laws that affect daily life—such as property taxes, school funding, and business regulations—are created and enforced at the state and local levels. Property taxes play a significant role in determining where people can afford to live, as higher property taxes can increase housing costs. Additionally, school funding is largely dependent on local and state government decisions, meaning that where you live directly impacts the quality of education your children receive. Since not all schools are created equally, some argue that participation in state and local elections is more important than national elections because these elections have a direct effect on daily life, dictating opportunities and access to resources in ways federal decisions may not.

While national politics gets the most attention, local government has a direct impact on daily life. Understanding how local leadership is structured is just as important as knowing what happens in Washington, D.C.

- **District Representatives** – Each city and county is divided into districts, with elected officials representing local communities. These officials influence city planning, education, and local policies.

- **State Legislature** – Each state has its own House and Senate, which create and vote on state laws. State legislatures handle issues like taxes, education funding, and infrastructure.

- **Governor** – The governor is the leader of a state, similar to how the president leads the country. Governors approve or veto state laws, manage state budgets, and oversee emergency responses.

Many laws that affect daily life—such as property taxes, school funding, and business regulations—are created and enforced at the state and local levels, making it essential for men to pay attention to these elections as well.

Where Looking for a Few Good Men: The Role of the Military

One of the key elements that solidifies America as a global superpower is its military strength. The ability to protect its own territory and that of its allies has positioned the United States as a dominant force in world affairs. Military presence extends beyond national defense; it also plays a crucial role in international diplomacy, humanitarian efforts, and crisis response.

The U.S. military is divided into several branches, each serving a distinct purpose:

- **Army** – The primary ground force responsible for land-based military operations.

- **Navy** – Conducts maritime warfare and maintains control of the seas.

- **Air Force** – Focuses on aerial and space superiority, including defense and surveillance.
- **Marine Corps** – Serves as a rapid-response force, specializing in amphibious and expeditionary warfare.
- **Coast Guard** – Ensures coastal security, drug interdiction, and search-and-rescue missions.
- **Space Force** – The newest branch, responsible for defending U.S. interests in space.

Participation in the military requires dedication, sacrifice, and discipline. Whether serving in combat roles or support positions, members of the armed forces contribute to the nation's security and global stability. Many who serve develop leadership skills, a strong work ethic, and a deep sense of duty.

It is important to acknowledge and thank those who have served or are currently serving. Their commitment ensures that the freedoms and opportunities available in America remain protected. Many of us have family members and friends who have served and are serving in the military and even fought in wars, making personal sacrifices for the greater good of the nation. Their dedication and bravery deserve recognition and appreciation.

Why This Matters for Men

Men are often expected to be leaders in their households and communities. Leadership requires awareness. Being politically informed doesn't mean becoming a politician; it means understanding how the system works and how it affects you. Laws impact job opportunities, taxes, healthcare, gun rights, and even family dynamics in areas like child support and custody battles.

Ignoring politics doesn't make it go away. I often hear people say they will do what they want regardless, believing that politicians are not truly for the people. After watching numerous debates and conducting hours of research, I have noticed that much of the rhetoric on both sides is divisive rather than unifying. Democrats push one agenda while Republicans push another, often leaving the average citizen feeling disconnected from true representation. However, understanding the system allows men to make informed decisions, vote wisely, and engage in discussions that directly impact their future and the well-being of their communities.

At the end of the day, don't rely on another man to put your family or community in the best position. The deeper you dive into politics, the more you realize that self-reliance is key. Government policies may change, but your ability to adapt, stay informed, and take control of your circumstances will always be the greatest asset in securing a better future for yourself and those who depend on you.

Political awareness is not about taking a pill to blindly follow one ideology; it's about knowing the facts, making educated choices, and taking control of the aspects of life that matter most.

MAKE THE CHURCH GREAT AGAIN

I want to talk about religion—or more specifically, the presentation of the belief in Jesus Christ and the idea that there is a God. This belief, or the concept of it, is presented to us in many forms, through various denominations and doctrines. It's much like chocolate, which comes in many varieties, yet its core is cocoa. You can't have real chocolate without cocoa.

Interestingly, I'm allergic to cocoa. As a child, I was never raised to know the difference between pure cocoa and imitation chocolate—I was simply told I was allergic, so I avoided all chocolate. One day, at Camp High Rock in Connecticut, I was introduced to s'mores. I ate two without realizing there was a piece of Hershey's chocolate in between. It was dark out, and I didn't notice until someone next to me dropped theirs. I pulled mine apart and saw the chocolate—and yet, I had no reaction.

It was later explained to me that what I ate wasn't pure chocolate. Still, my mother insisted I avoid it altogether—it wasn't worth the risk of not knowing what's real and what's imitation. I've never knowingly eaten it since.

Religion today feels similar—so many imitation messages with little to no real reaction or impact on the listener. Sure, the experience may feel good. The music may be moving. The energy in the room may lift your spirit. But when you encounter the **pure word**—the message that is well-studied, deeply understood, and accurately interpreted—there's a profound reaction. A lasting impact. A real transformation.

Somewhere along the line, the church has drifted from the purity of the Word. In an attempt to reach more people, some leaders have diluted the message. But here's the truth: a message that lacks hope and sustainability is like a product that looks good on the shelf but fails when put to use.

Let me explain how I arrived at this controversial subject. I've come to view the church through the lens of business—because in many ways, that's how it functions. Most churches today are structured like organizations, and this becomes especially clear in the operations of mega churches. With that in mind, if we're going to view the church as a business, then we also have to ask: what is the service being offered? What is the product being delivered?

Let's talk about religion as a product. Every product is attached to some sense of hope—hope for change, improvement, relief, or transformation. After enough use of any product, one or two things happen: you either get tired of it, or you become addicted to it. Most products evolve to keep your interest. And if you get bored with one brand, you switch to another offering the same substance, just a different manufacturer. In this case, a different church.

We now have spiritual consumerism. Churches cater to preferences instead of convictions. Believers are addicted to the *experience* of church, but untouched by the substance of God. And when the church becomes a performance, the people become spectators, not participants.

Let me put this disclaimer out: I am a believer in Jesus Christ. I believe in the Trinity and in the teachings of the Bible. However, I'll be honest—I still wrestle with some theological concepts. I'm not entirely convinced that there is only one understanding of God, but I do believe that Jesus is the Son of the God I serve. That belief anchors me.

Now, let me address something else—I don't subscribe to the concept of hope as it's commonly sold. For me, hope either is or it isn't. Life isn't always black or white, I understand that, and I recognize the gray areas. But this trend of "hope campaigns" doesn't sit well with me. Either you will or you won't. You did or you didn't. You want to, or you don't. That's how I process things. I prefer clarity, not empty optimism.

I acknowledge that I'm a sinner—and I emphasize the "-er" because it's not past tense. I will sin again. In fact, it's possible I'm sinning right now in thought, word, or deed. But the difference is this: I know it. I own it. God knows my heart, my intentions, and I'm thankful for grace through Jesus Christ—even if I still have questions about some parts of the story. And if you don't have any questions about your faith journey, I'm actually a little concerned for you. Faith should spark curiosity, not just conformity.

Now that I've gotten that out of the way, let's continue with the conversation. This isn't about questioning for the sake of rebellion—it's about pursuing a deeper, more honest relationship with God. If faith is supposed to be a journey, then we should be prepared to walk through the questions, not avoid them. So, let's keep going—with reverence, with transparency, and with the desire to build something real.

Church Shaming

Another issue is the subtle shame that still surrounds religion and church culture. I was raised to believe there was a divide—those who went to church were seen as good and righteous, and those who didn't were automatically viewed as lost or wayward. That judgmental mindset hasn't gone anywhere; in fact, it still shows up in some of the most personal spaces in our lives. Families break ties over differing beliefs. Spouses disagree about church participation to the point that it causes division in the household—even separation in the bedroom.

People use scripture not as a tool for spiritual growth, but as ammunition in arguments—with friends, with family, even within marriages. Instead of fostering peace and understanding, the Word is used as a weapon to win a debate or prove superiority. That's not what it was meant for. And that misuse only deepens the shame and pushes people further from the very faith they're being judged by.

Then there's the flawed notion that if you find your spouse in church, they must be the one. That sounds noble—but limiting. The Bible says, "He who finds a wife finds a good thing," not that she must be found within the four walls of a sanctuary. This oversimplified teaching has led many into relationships that were more religiously convenient than spiritually compatible.

In the same way, if you're a believer, you're often viewed as uptight or judgmental, someone out of touch with reality. There's a stereotype that Christians are stiff-necked or not relatable. How many times have you heard someone say, "Aren't you supposed to be a Christian?"—usually after they've crossed a line or mistreated you. As if being a Christian means you're supposed to tolerate anything and everything without response. But let's be clear: being a believer doesn't mean you're a doormat. Grace and boundaries can coexist.

Just like chocolate comes in various wrappers, so does the church. Once faith hits the public, it's dressed up in branding, programs, titles, and rituals. But underneath it all, is the Word pure? Are we still tasting what is real—or have we settled for flavor without substance?

Just to be clear, I'm talking specifically about the church—its structure, its influence, and the role it plays in the community—not the broader and more diverse concept of religion. There are many different religious beliefs in the world, but the church often becomes the common space where those beliefs are introduced, taught, and explored. The issue is that, for many, the learning stops at theory. There's very little practice, very little application. We gather in the space, hear the words, sing the songs—but how much are we truly living out what we say we believe? That's why I'm making this distinction. There's a deeper reason I've drawn this line, and I promise to unpack it fully as we continue.

Pulpit Bully: The Interpreter's Dilemma

Every party has a hype man, an MC, let's address the pulpit. The orator—the minister, pastor, bishop, or interpreter of the gospel—is meant to deliver truth, not performance. But many of today's leaders have diluted the message to make it palatable to all, ensuring everyone gets a taste, but few experience lasting transformation. It's like scratching off a lottery ticket—keep showing up, and maybe you'll win.

Instead of empowering people to seek God for sustainable solutions—spiritually, financially, emotionally—we've defaulted to offering momentary inspiration. It might feel good in the moment, but without substance and follow-through, it's fleeting. That's not the gospel; that's emotional gambling—betting that a feel-good moment will carry someone through a lifetime of challenges without giving them the tools to navigate real life with faith and discipline.

How do we get the church back to this level of impact, you ask?

Teach, Teach, and Teach.

Teach how to manage money

Teach how to invest money

teach how to recognize conflict

Teach conflict resolution

Teach how to start a business

Teach how to use cell phones

Teach how to do taxes

Teach how to gain life insurance

Teach how to drive

Teach how to complete job applications

TEACH DAMMIT!!!!

Clickbait Ministry

We now live in a world shaped by social media, and like any tool, it comes with its pros and cons—especially when it comes to the church. One of the major benefits is that sermons and services can now be livestreamed and archived online. This advancement has allowed ministers and churches to reach more people than ever before, and for many, it's opened the door to salvation and connection to Christ, which is the ultimate goal.

But on the flip side, social media also shines a light on the cracks in the foundation. It exposes flawed doctrines, performative preaching, and questionable theology to the masses. Messages that lack sound biblical study are no longer hidden within the walls of a single church—they're shared, reposted, and critiqued across platforms. The doctrine is being tested in real time by a wider, often more informed audience.

What used to be tolerated in the local church now faces global scrutiny. And while that accountability can be good, it also means the church must move from entertainment to education, from emotion to truth, and from popularity to purpose. Because the platform might be bigger, but the responsibility is greater too. Many interpreters of the Gospel seem to have a start complex, and then it becomes more about who is delivering the message as opposed to the message that is being delivered. I once asked my mom what if, after a sermon there was a test to see what we had actually comprehended and understood?

Staple in the Community

The church can be a powerful and multifaceted force in the community—and it used to be. Across cultures and geographic regions, the church played different roles depending on the needs of the people. In parts of the South, famously known as the Bible Belt, the church had a significant influence on local laws and served as a central place for organizing and advocating for justice. It was one of the most populated and trusted gathering places. And like any business or institution rooted in the community, the church also bore a unique responsibility to care for that community, arguably more than any other organization.

In many cases, the church is the oldest institution in a neighborhood. Generations have passed through its doors. Entire family legacies have been shaped from those pews. Children found their voices through church plays and recitations. They gained confidence, leadership skills, and public speaking experience within those walls. These experiences helped mold many of us into the people we are today.

Today, however, it feels like that level of consistency, effort, and reliability has faded. Many churches still serve, but the frequency and intensity of their community involvement have noticeably lessened.

Let's be specific: food and clothing giveaways used to be consistent—year-round support, not just around holidays. Now it seems like acts of service are occasional events, often reserved for Thanksgiving or Christmas. While seasonal generosity is great, what about the other ten months of the year? People still need to eat. Children still outgrow their clothes. The church once understood this and met the need consistently.

I know this topic may cause discomfort, so let me be clear: if this message speaks to you, receive it. If it doesn't, pass it along to someone; it might help. The point is simple: the church was once a dependable, transformative, service-minded presence in the community. Not just on Sundays, but all week long. It's time to return to that kind of intentional, consistent outreach.

It would be incomplete and irresponsible for me to bring up these concerns without acknowledging the possibility that interest in the church may genuinely be fading. Maybe the proverbial gig is up. Maybe people are looking for more than just a feel-good song and a motivational speech. Maybe this is why pews are empty in some sanctuaries. Could it be that today's churchgoers feel spiritually lost, not because of what's outside the church, but because of what's lacking within?

So how do we measure progress? How does the church define growth? Is it purely by the number of members who join, or by how many convert to Christ or a particular belief system? Those metrics have their place, but I'd like to offer another suggestion: what if we measured growth by the individual progress of the people in the pews? What if the real metric were how lives are changed, not just how services are attended?

Imagine if churches began offering intentional workshops and focused messages tailored to the specific needs of their congregation—whether that be addiction, financial literacy, mental health, or single parenting. What if outreach efforts extended beyond general acts of kindness and focused on the core needs within a 3–5-mile radius of the church itself?

I know some of these things are already being done in some churches, but it's hard to quantify because the data is often skewed, inconsistent, or undocumented. A better method? Ride around the neighborhood. Walk the streets. Ask the people nearby if they feel the presence and impact of that church in their community. You're either having an effect—or you're not.

Outreach isn't optional. It's vital. The church must meet people where they are, not just expect them to walk through the doors. One reason some people avoid the church is because of the stigma that "church folk" act superior. As I mentioned earlier, this idea of church shaming—of judging those who don't attend or believe the same—has hurt more than it's helped. It's not a tactful or effective way to draw anyone in.

It's time we shifted our focus from appearances to action, from performance to purpose, from numbers to transformation.

Don't Be So Hard on the Church... But Be Honest

If you're still reading and haven't closed the book or judged me harshly for this critique, let me say this: **we must hold the church accountable—because our communities depend on it.** There should be one Church, one God, and one people. But like chocolate, once it hits the shelves, it's wrapped in countless packages. Let me go a little further because I want you to finish reading this book.

We've traded spiritual nourishment for emotional experiences. Many believers don't know how to pray because they're always being prayed for. They don't know how to fast effectively because they're only instructed to do it once a year. They don't know how to seek God for themselves because they're constantly being called to the altar.

It's time to get real. As men, we must seek first the kingdom of God and let all these other things be added unto us. There was a time when we did that—when the world was more spiritually grounded. Now, our flesh runs wild while our spirits grow malnourished.

Let's make the Church great again—not by going back to tradition, but by going back to truth.

AUDIBLE

Audible: The Power of Change

Webster's Dictionary defines "audible" in three ways. The first, as an adjective, means "heard or capable of being heard." The second, as a noun, refers to "a substitute offensive or defensive play called at the line of scrimmage." The third, as a verb, means "to call an audible."

This second definition is what I'd like to focus on.

When discussing audibles in football, there's no better example than the great Thomas Edward Patrick Brady Jr.—better known as Tom Brady. Arguably the greatest quarterback in NFL history, Brady played in 10 Super Bowls, winning six with the New England Patriots and one with the Tampa Bay Buccaneers. He shattered records and, at first glance, may have seemed like any other quarterback. But for those who never watched him play or don't follow football, let me illustrate what made him so great in my eyes.

The Quarterback: A Leader of Men

The quarterback position is one of great responsibility. Beyond throwing an accurate pass or executing a handoff, a quarterback must be a leader. He is the voice his teammates hear in the huddle, the one who receives communication from the sidelines, and the one who looks his teammates in the eyes to gauge their focus and readiness.

Every offensive play starts with the quarterback. Whether he hands the ball off to a running back or drops back to throw, the defense's objective is clear: sack him before he can throw or anticipate the run and swarm the ball carrier. A quarterback has mere seconds to make a decision once the ball is snapped—usually, that decision is made even before the play begins. If all else fails, he can try to run the ball himself, though not every quarterback is built for that role.

Man's Greatest Weapon

Tom Brady was never known for his speed or ability to escape the pocket. What made him elite was his ability to read the defense, recognize what was coming, and fearlessly call an audible at the line of scrimmage.

Brady knew that once the ball was snapped, he had roughly 3-5 seconds to make a decision. He wasn't going to outrun defenders, so he perfected his ability to outthink them. He studied film relentlessly, recognizing defensive tendencies and formations. He had the best vantage point, standing directly behind the center, looking into the eyes of the defense, and adjusting accordingly.

Ray Lewis, the legendary linebacker of the Baltimore Ravens, once said, **"Playing against Brady is like playing chess."**

That's exactly what made Brady special—he was always thinking several moves ahead. He was unafraid to scrap the original plan, recognizing when a better opportunity presented itself. His teammates and coaches trusted him completely, knowing he would put them in the best possible position to succeed.

Audible in Life

Brady's ability to call audibles serves as a powerful metaphor for life. As men, as leaders—whether in our careers, relationships, or personal growth—we cannot be afraid to change the play.

Sometimes, life calls for an audible. Maybe you need to switch careers, move to a new city, or make a tough decision for your family. Like Brady, preparation is key: study, analyze, and then make the right call. If you're a husband or father, your family is counting on you to read the situation and adjust when necessary.

Not every play will be perfect. Even Brady, with all his greatness, went to the Super Bowl 10 times and won 7. That means he lost 3 times—but he's still considered the greatest of all time.

So, don't fear calling an audible. Make the necessary adjustments, gain positive yards in life, and keep moving forward.

CULTURE

The word *culture* originates from the Latin word *cultura*, meaning to grow or cultivate. At its root is the word *cult*—not in the modern negative sense we associate with extremism, but in its original meaning: a shared system of beliefs, rituals, and values. When expanded upon, *culture* becomes the collective habits, language, customs, food, music, and expressions that define a group of people. It shapes how we live, how we relate, and how we pass down our values from one generation to the next.

Culture is the glue of community. Whether it's the culture of your neighborhood, your heritage, or your profession, it impacts your identity. In our communities and cities, we see culture in the foods cooked in home kitchens, the sports kids play after school, the music blasting from cars, and the language painted in murals on brick walls. Each part represents someone's story.

Sports teams often blend cultures in a way that fosters unity—players of different races and backgrounds come together under one common goal: to win. It doesn't matter if one guy is from Brooklyn and the other from Brazil. What matters is their shared mission and the respect built through effort, discipline, and teamwork. The same is true in kitchens where culinary traditions from Mexico, Ethiopia, Korea, and Italy can find harmony in a single dish.

Entertainment is one of the greatest forces of cultural fusion. In music, you'll find hip-hop sampling soul, jazz weaving into pop, and Latin rhythms infiltrating global dance charts. Movies do the same through characters and storytelling. Sylvester Stallone's roles in *Rocky* and *Rambo* merged the cultures of masculinity, Italian American heritage, and military grit. Al Pacino portrayed the weight of tradition and power in *The Godfather*, bringing mob culture into the public imagination.

Music venues, arenas, and even street corners become sacred spaces where strangers unite over sound. Race, gender, and age fade in the face of shared rhythm. And on a smaller scale, I've witnessed culture up close as a carpenter and business owner, working alongside people from around the world. My friend Junior, a Jamaican man, brings stories, work ethic, and curried chicken to the lunch table. That's culture in action.

Social media is now one of the loudest cultural influences. It can unite or divide, inform or mislead. Trends spread fast, sometimes becoming movements and sometimes just distractions. Culture is now not just local—it's digital and global. We must remain mindful of what we consume, share, and believe.

Then there are the cultural differences between regions, like the South and the North. Southern culture leans into hospitality, faith, family, and food. Northern culture often moves faster, values independence, and speaks bluntly. Both have strengths. Both have shortcomings. But when they meet, there's room for growth.

Still, nothing has been distorted more than race culture. Society has used race to divide rather than to inspire curiosity, connection, and mutual respect. We've used skin color to judge rather than to learn. Why is it that as men, we can bond over our favorite sports team at a bar, but not over our shared manhood?

Closing Reflection

If I've proven anything through this writing, it's this: regardless of race, age, or background, every man faces the same core challenges: taking responsibility, practicing discipline, seeking awareness, and being held accountable.

Awareness is key, awareness that the man who doesn't look like you probably has more in common with you than you think. Maybe he grew up rich, and you grew up poor. Maybe he has a college degree, while you built your life through a trade. Maybe he's married with kids, and you're still finding your way alone. Maybe he believes differently, votes, or lives in a different part of town.

But none of that means you can't sit with him over a beer and a prayer. The truth is most of us are walking the same road in different shoes.

Culture, class, education, or relationship status — none of these should be barriers. They should be bridges.

Because at the end of the day, being a man isn't about where you come from or what you have — it's about who you are, how you carry yourself, and how you treat others along the way.

Author's Reflection

Now that I'm a man, I see things through a wider lens. Time, experience, and faith have a way of shaping how you view strength, purpose, and peace. The older I get, the clearer it becomes—**it truly takes a lot to be a man.** It takes patience, discipline, accountability, and a willingness to keep growing no matter how much you think you already know.

I've learned that our differences—race, background, or belief—were never meant to divide us. They were meant to teach us. Every man carries his own version of struggle, yet when you strip away the surface, our challenges look very much the same. We all want to be respected. We all want peace in our homes, purpose in our work, and love that lasts.

To some, what I'm saying might not seem believable, because race *has* divided us. I understand that fully. I've seen it, felt it, and lived it. I'm aware of the overplay of it, and the stronghold it can still have on people through pain and generational trauma. I don't deny the weight of it. I just choose not to let it define or divide me or hold me back. Where there is a will, there will remain a way. My story has its share of those experiences, and I carry them with awareness—not bitterness. They remind me that healing and understanding take work, not walls.

Some have had it easier because of their race, some have inherited more, and some have been given opportunities others never had. The truth is, many have not. So, do I continue living and making excuses? Will you? I choose to move toward a greater place—with purpose, awareness, and understanding.

As an African American author, I want to make it clear—this is not about the race of man. This is a deeper perspective about **the being and becoming** of a man, through *all* races of men. The message is not color-bound; it's character-bound. Every man, regardless of where he starts, has to make the same choice: to grow, to lead, and to live with integrity.

Manhood isn't a destination—it's a process. It's not something you arrive at; it's something you practice every day. When I was younger, I thought being a man meant being in control, staying silent, and showing no weakness. Over time, I realized real strength comes from restraint, humility, and self-awareness. A man who understands himself can lead others with wisdom.

The truth is, what connects us as men runs deeper than what separates us. The man across from you might look different, live different, or believe different, yet he's often fighting a battle you know all too well. We just rarely talk about it.

Now that I'm a man, I know that growth doesn't end—it evolves. Every season brings new lessons, new responsibilities, and new chances to improve. The key is to stay teachable, to stay grounded, and to never let pride close your heart to learning.

Through this book, another man may see a reflection of himself—not as someone behind, rather as someone *becoming.* We're all working to carry the load a little better each day.

When men grow, families grow. When families grow, communities grow. And when communities grow, culture changes.

It takes a lot to be a man.
It's worth every step of the journey.
So keep your hand on the plow—because the work of becoming never ends.

Until me and this pen meet again – THE END.

www.ingramcontent.com/pod-product-compliance
Lightning Source LLC
LaVergne TN
LVHW090940080826
845145LV00003B/831

9781737108030